I LOVE
YOU
&
I LIKE
YOU

I LOVE YOU & I LIKE YOU

STEVE & ANNIE CHAPMAN

HARVEST HOUSE PUBLISHERS
EUGENE, OREGON

Cover photo © iStockphoto / Thinkstock

Cover by Koechel Peterson & Associates, Inc., Minneapolis, Minnesota

I LOVE YOU AND I LIKE YOU
Copyright © 1989; updated 2013 by Steve and Annie Chapman
Published 2014 by Harvest House Publishers
Eugene, Oregon 97402
www.harvesthousepublishers.com

Library of Congress Cataloging-in-Publication Data
Chapman, Steve.
   [Growing together as lovers and friends]
   I love you and I like you / Steve and Annie Chapman.
      pages cm
   Rev. ed. of: Growing together as lovers and friends.
   ISBN 978-0-7369-5527-0 (pbk.)
   ISBN 978-0-7369-5528-7 (eBook)
   1. Marriage—Religious aspects—Christianity. I. Title.
   BV835.C4595 2013
   248.8'44—dc23

                                          2013016742

Printed in the United States of America

13 14 15 16 17 18 19 20 21 22 / BP-JH / 10 9 8 7 6 5 4 3 2 1

To our parents:
Paul J. and Lillian M. Chapman
and
N.R. and Sylvia A. Williamson
They modeled love, commitment, and sacrifice for
their children, grandchildren, and great-grandchildren.
They taught us that we can be married
and still remain friends.

And to our children and their spouses:
Nathan and Stephanie Chapman
and
Heidi and Emmitt Beall

Contents

Love Doesn't Have to Wane!

by Annie

When the evening started, neither Steve nor I expected we'd end it glaring at each other. And, embarrassingly enough, the issue we feuded over wasn't something as major as money, or mothers-in-law, or the lack of world peace. We wound up filling the room with emotional icicles over—well, you won't believe it…

The evening began innocently enough. Our family was eagerly tuning-in to watch the Summer Olympics. At least Steve and our children were. I'm not much of a sports enthusiast. I knew it was my duty as a patriot to watch the games, so I joined Steve and the kids in the family room. The advantage as well as the disadvantage of having only one TV in the house is that our family was forced to watch the same show. I sat down beside my beloved Steve and forced an interest in the games.

A few minutes passed, and I found my loyalty drifting. Then I saw it. There it was on the table—the scepter of authority powered by two AA batteries. The remote control. I knew it could salvage my evening. I picked it up and, with power in hand, waited for a commercial. As soon as it came on, I searched for other entertainment options. As I flipped through the channels, I happened upon an old movie I'd wanted to see for awhile. Two channels later, I found a documentary highlighting a pressing national issue I thought I ought to be informed about. Just before moving back to the platform diving competition, I paused at one of our family's favorite sitcoms.

We'd barely started watching the sitcom when a commercial interrupted. Not wanting to waste time hearing a sales pitch for a car I didn't need, I touched a button on the remote and switched over to the documentary to catch a moment or two. As soon as the documentary went to commercial, I flipped back to the Olympics.

The network was covering the equestrian competition, which wasn't big in our family and didn't interest me at all. I knew the documentary would still be in the midst of commercials, so I once again punched the remote and found the sitcom.

It only took a minute or two for me to realize I'd seen this episode before, so I zapped the channel over to see how the movie was progressing.

"Annie, we were watching the Olympics," Steve complained.

"Yeah, I know," I said as I nodded, my eyes glued to the set. "We'll get back to it in a minute. I just need to see how this movie starts so I'll know what's happening if the Olympics don't get more interesting." I watched for a minute or two. Satisfied, I flipped to the documentary. (These are moments when an uncanny sense of just how long a commercial will last comes in handy.) We caught what, to me, was a key list of statistics. When they started droning on about "sociological implications," I cut away to the sitcom.

"Annie!" Steve's voice had taken on a harder edge. "The Olympics!"

"They've finished all the good stuff," I explained to him as patiently as I could, which wasn't easy because I was trying to remember what happened next in the sitcom so I could decide whether or not this would be a good time to check in again on the Olympics.

That was it. Steve went for the remote control in my hand.

But he didn't understand that I have the mental capability of watching five shows at the same time while keeping them all straight in my head. He also didn't realize how quickly I can move when someone goes for the remote.

Steve and I often lead seminars on marriage, so in the interest of preserving a portion of our credibility, I'll spare you a jab-by-jab account of the argument that followed. You'll probably get the picture if I tell you that later that night, when the news ironically reported a man killed his girlfriend in a tussle over their remote control, Steve got a knowing gleam in his eye. (He was probably remembering what Mrs. Billy Graham once said when she was asked whether she'd ever considered divorce: "No, but I've thought of murder!")

Later, when Steve and I were speaking to each other again, we both realized how silly and thoughtless we'd been toward each other.

We Know We're Not Alone

Arguments like this are typical of married couples everywhere. Like you, we shouted our "I do's" from hearts bursting with love and hopes as high as the late-March sun that brightened our wedding day. But add a few years, house payments, 15 extra pounds, two kids, and too much to do, and, well, let's say we've seen firsthand how compromise and forgiveness must work in a healthy marriage. Two people can start out in love and wind up bitter enemies unless they take action to keep love and friendship growing.

On one concert trip, a couple picked us up at the airport to take us to the church where we were to sing. To get to know the husband and wife, we made polite conversation. Steve asked the husband, "How long have the two of you been married?" Without missing a beat, the husband responded, "Eleven years—but it feels like eleven days…without any sleep."

We soon learned the husband was quite the quick-witted jokester and was only being funny. But for some couples being married for many years may not be a laughing matter. That's not what God wants. He wants our marriages to be fulfilling, loving, satisfying.

We laugh because we all know at least one marriage like that. God never intended matrimony to wear the shine off a love affair. He designed marital oneness as a haven where love can blossom into its full beauty. He intended that husbands and wives be "in love" and "in like" all their lives.

In the pages ahead, Steve and I invite you to join us in a journey toward making our marriages all that God intended. As we share our struggles, we hope you'll feel less alone in your daily squabbles. We hope too that as you see some directives the Lord has given us for growing together, you'll come away with increased faith and ideas to make your marriage even more dynamic.

Love doesn't have to wane or die. Like us, you will discover that your marriage can continually improve and remain vital with God's ever-present help. In fact, the two of you may rediscover an excitement in your relationship that rekindles the passion and vibrancy you felt when you were newlyweds.

1

A Decision to Make

by Steve

*D*uring my daze in skool, spelling wuz never my best corse. But when someone asks me to spell "love," it's a word I'm sure to get right. Real love has to consist of T-I-M-E. You can't build a relationship with anyone unless you continue to spend *time* together. People know that instinctively when they're dating, but when they marry they seem to assume time together is no longer necessary. Nothing could be further from the truth! But this was a lesson I had to learn the hard way.

When Annie and I got married, I was a traveling musician. This proved to be no detriment to our bliss because I had the good sense to choose a woman who could sing like an angel, who understood my ministry, and who wanted to make it her ministry as well. Annie just threw her suitcase into the van, and off we went. We didn't have to make any major choices, so we could give each other all the time we wanted. We could roll on with life, each doing what we did best and still find ourselves together nearly 24 hours a day. And we'd both had enough relational experience to know how to use the time we had to build strong, loving bonds between us. (We'll talk more about that later—what to *do* with the time together to make it even more worthwhile.)

So the Chapmans were happily chugging down the highway of life. After all this time together, not surprisingly, Annie became pregnant, so we knew some changes were in the offing.

Nathan's arrival forced us to think over what kind of life God wanted for our family. One thing we believed was that God didn't intend our children to be an afterthought, crammed here and there in the crannies of our schedules. We'd known people who left their children behind when they took to the road, using rationales like "the importance of God's work" and "quality time is what matters not quantity time." But Annie and I knew God hadn't given us a child so someone else could raise him. We also believed ministering to *our* family was every bit as important to God as our ministry to other families.

We decided together that I'd go on with the group and Annie would stay home with Nathan. Though Annie and I knew we'd miss each other terribly, she viewed parenting as the high calling of God it is. She didn't believe she could do a good job mothering while traveling so much, so having her settle in at home seemed like the best way to go.

When Annie left the group, it took no less than a 5-piece band to replace her. With 7 families to support, the group had to be on the road 15 to 20 days a month just to meet expenses. I found myself gone from my wife and child 75 percent of the time.

In those early years of parenting, the advantages of communication technology for the home were still at least a decade away. There were no cell phones, tablets, or Facebook and other social media websites. Texting and Skyping hadn't been invented to help us feel connected. To ease the pain of my absence, I did what I could to stay close to Annie and Nathan. I'd find a pay phone and call home every day. I worked hard at sending cards and letters while I was gone so they'd know how much I was thinking of them. And when I was home, I'd try to compensate by making our time together special.

You Have My Word

You have my heart; it's yours alone
You have my soul 'til time is gone
But there's one thing of greater worth
I give it now; you have my word

You have my word, I promise you
Long as I live, I will be true
Your love is more than I deserve
I'll hold it close; you have my word

You have my hopes and all my dreams
You have my years—all that remain
Still there's one thing of greater worth
You have it now; I give my word

You have my word, I promise you
Long as I live, I will be true
Your love is more than I deserve
I'll hold it close; you have my word [1]

Annie worked hard to make a go of it too. Because she didn't want to stand in the way of my work and ministry, she cheerily pushed me out the door on the days I'd have to go. What she didn't tell me was that as soon as the door closed behind me, she'd head for the bathroom and throw up due to anxiety and sadness. She didn't tell me either that while I traveled, her periods stopped. And she didn't let me know about the many nights she cried herself to sleep from loneliness.

Our son also started showing the effects of his daddy's long absences. We made jokes about Nathan learning his numbers by counting the days till his dad came home, but to a little child it was no laughing matter. He was learning that his dad wasn't a real parent to be counted on. Once when I was home and reprimanded him, he shot back, "Old man, why don't you just get back in that motorhome and go on another trip?" Corrections that meant something came from his mom, not from this shadowy figure who appeared now and then.

If there ever was a moment in our lives when we looked like the typical American couple, this was it. Husband giving his best energy to earning a living; wife giving her best energy to raising the kids; the home little more than a refueling station and message center. In fact, we knew a couple who never fought…because they were *never* together long enough. And we weren't far from being just like them. Annie and I chose to live like this from wonderful Christian motives, but the toll it was taking on our marriage and family was great.

And I felt miserable. How could I do the ministry I felt God had given me and still give the quality and quantity time I felt my family needed? I pleaded with God for a better answer than the one we were living. Little by little I began to realize I had a decision to make. Would my family have to accommodate my work…or was work going to accommodate my family? When I understood that God intended my family to be my first priority after Him and before making a living, I knew I'd have to leave the band. So while on the road with the group in Illinois, I broke the news to the guys that I was giving my six-month notice.

From a human standpoint, this decision was one of the scariest things I've ever done. In one fell swoop I cut myself off from my source of employment, my income, and my career for the sake of my family. As the band drove back to Nashville that night, I had about as much tranquility as a man facing a firing squad. Was I doing the right thing?

We arrived home early Sunday morning, and since Annie had already left for Sunday school, I asked the guys to drop me off at our church. I trudged into the building loaded down with all the fears and questions that only a man who has just quit his job and has no prospects for the future can understand. Fortunately, our Sunday school class was watching a film so the room was dark. At least Annie wouldn't be able to see the worry on my face when I walked in. Just as I stepped into our classroom and slid into a seat beside my wife, the man on the screen looked straight at me (or at least that's how it seemed) and said pointedly, "How can you be a good husband and father if you're never home?" Honest! Those were his exact words.

At that second, I knew in my "heart of hearts" that I *was* doing the right thing. My decision might mean I'd have to find a job that would take me away from the stage, but that sacrifice would be small compared to the fulfillment of knowing I was finally making my wife and child the high priority the Lord wanted them to be.

Can you guess what happened next? On the scene bursts a big-time producer from a hot-selling gospel record company. He offered Annie and me a big-bucks contract and our own Nashville recording studio, complete with backup singers and an adjoining nursery. Okay, that's not exactly how it went.

I took a low-paying slot in a jingle company writing advertising ditties. We scratched along on just enough to meet expenses. We were scraping by on that front, but Annie and I made up for lost time emotionally and spiritually as we learned how to give our relationship the attention the Lord intended it to have.

I was still able to do some singing on the side. As I did, the desire began to fester to have Annie singing with me. I knew the kind of musical gift she'd been given, and I felt increasingly frustrated that it wasn't being used. Annie, however, wasn't the least bit concerned. She knew God had called her to be a mom, so a mom was what she was content to be. By now little Heidi had come into our lives. With my urging, Annie finally agreed to try singing together occasionally—just to please me, I'm sure.

Everything we did, the Lord seemed to smile on. God stirred in Annie, prodding her toward considering the possibility that even though He wanted us together, it might not be in our little house in Nashville. She began to wonder if maybe He was saying we should take to the road—and bring the kids with us.

Saying yes to this idea was every bit as scary for Annie as leaving the band had been for me. But because of her commitment to the Lord and to the priority of our marriage, she finally agreed to give it a try. We packed up our young'uns in a blue van, our equipment in a little trailer, and off we went. The rest, as they say, is history.

Of course, in most history books you hear more about the triumphs than you do the tragedies. In our case, living crammed in a van with a preschooler and a baby leaned far more heavily to the side of tragedy—or hilarity, depending on how we chose to look at it.

For instance, there was one time when we nearly ruined our welcome at a huge church in Texas…

If you've been through the toilet-training phase of raising children, you know this is one arena where the trainee calls all the shots. When he's gotta go, he's gotta go. To accommodate Nathan and nature's beckoning, we plunked a potty chair in the middle of the van. It served its purpose, but to make the trip bearable we'd empty the thing as soon as we stopped.

This particular time, we pulled up to a church in Texas where we were scheduled to perform. I was assigned potty chair cleanup duty. I needed to do some other things, so I talked Annie into doing the dreaded chore. She picked the chair up and headed for the church to find a restroom. All would have gone well, except she forgot she wasn't dealing with our old, familiar chair. We'd left the other one sitting on top of our equipment trailer on our last trip, and when we drove off it slid off and smashed on the cement. We'd made a quick stop at a well-known box store to acquire a replacement. This chair didn't have a safety bar in the back to hold the bowl in place like our old one had. Thus, a disaster was in the making.

Annie wrangled open the heavy church door with her fingers and then her hip. Just as she stepped inside and swung around, the bowl slid out of the back of the potty chair and landed upside down on the floor. It looked like she'd opened the door and deliberately emptied the unsavory contents inside. She realized quickly that the hall had been newly carpeted!

Much to her relief, all the foul stuff "just happened" to land right in the middle of a large, plastic mat positioned inside the door. *Whew!* An innocent-looking teenaged boy also "just happened" to be sweeping the stairs nearby. Annie exchanged looks of horror with him. With a tone of intense urgency in her voice, she enlisted his help.

"Grab that end of the mat!" she commanded.

In stunned silence, he reluctantly picked up one end while Annie took the other. They slowly navigated the sloshy, smelly cargo to the restroom. Unbelievably, not a drop of it spilled.

We later found out the pastor was so protective of the new carpet that he wouldn't let people drink coffee in that part of the church lest they spill and soil the rug. Imagine the warm feelings he would have experienced toward the traveling musicians if he'd discovered they'd splashed his precious carpet with... Oh my.

The awful potty chair experience was a real test of our determination to travel together as a family. Actually, it was just one of many. Another moment of testing came when we read a review of one of our early recordings. The critic wrote, "The Chapmans sound like two soloists who just happen to be singing the same song at the same time." He was pointing out that our blend wasn't as easy to listen to as it should have been. Unhappily, he was right. Annie and I did have two voices that sounded better alone because learning to blend hadn't been a high priority for us yet. What the critic didn't know was that if we'd put music first in our lives, we wouldn't have worked together professionally.

The less-than-favorable record review caused us to reaffirm our belief that God intends our work to adapt to our marriage and not the other way around. To fix the duet harmony problem, we *learned* to sing together. And just like the other parts of our married life, practice has helped us find better ways to blend and produce sweeter music.

Although Spendy, Unity Is Worth It

Anything nice has its price. Part of the cost we Christians pay to put our marriages and families first is to be out-of-sync with the rest of the world. In the short term, there may not be many obvious rewards for being out of step. If you've struggled to get your priorities in order, you can take comfort in the fact that many others have faced the same dilemma and thrived.

Giving up other things to be at home sometimes doesn't pay off as we might expect. To illustrate this reality, here is a letter sent to us by a father who decided to take a stab at making his family a higher priority:

> During [your] concert I determined to spend the next day, Saturday, my day off, playing with my children (ages 6, 3, and 1½) all day. I was up coloring and building block houses much earlier than I expected. At 10:00 AM we were still going strong. My 18-month-old son was about to knock down my 6-year-old son's castle. I scooped up my 18-month-old son and, instead of shutting him out of the fun behind a gate, I remembered your concert and playfully swooped him up onto my head and twirled him around the room.
>
> It was at that moment my wife walked in and informed me that my 18-month-old son, who was sitting on my head, had a load in his pants that was soaking into my hair. My nose said she wasn't lying.
>
> I passed him to my wife, sprinted for the bathroom, jumped in the shower, turned on the water…and found

only cold water due to my wife doing loads of laundry that morning. As I stood there freezing, I wondered if this was the "family fun" you had spoken about the night before…

The pressure is on us to have it all, do it all, and be it all. And though I feel this pressure as a man, Annie reminds me of how exceptionally difficult it is right now for women to stand against the tide of rising expectations that tend to take us away from each other. She insists that if a person compiled a profile of the "perfect woman" from television, magazines, and talk shows, she'd look like this:

> She'd be a beautiful, alluring woman who constantly fulfills all her husband's fantasies, as well as her own. She's also a wonderfully devoted mother who finds her "quality time" with her children always in great quantity. Her children never have dirt on their faces, never eat just peanut butter sandwiches for lunch, never get served the heel of the bread, don't wear hand-me-down clothes, and always make straight A's and play the cello. Her home, of course, looks like the centerfold of *Southern Living* magazine.

> For *this* woman there's no ordinary job outside the home. She's lunging up the corporate ladder in an exciting career. Her job may demand 70 hours a week, but she always comes home looking fresh and beautiful.

> In her off hours, she serves as councilwoman for her district and president of the PTA. She bakes cookies for all the school functions, volunteers for the class field trips, sings in the church choir, and teaches Sunday school. Of course, she fits in workouts at the spa five days a week so she looks like a walking Diet Coke commercial. And while she's shrinking her waistline, she's also expanding her mind by taking law courses at the university.

Annie says, "Isn't it too bad that we Christians buy into this neurotic frenzy? We pull out Proverbs 31 and use it to beat women into quaking masses of guilt by insisting it's *spiritual* to have such impossible standards of achievement. We use the woman Solomon describes in Proverbs 31 to turn Superwoman into a saint." Annie also said, "The truth is that I used to hate the Proverbs 31 woman. She's beautiful, strong, well-organized, maternal, matrimonial, and managerial all at the same time. It's a load that seems too great for any person to carry."

But Annie has made her peace with this capable woman. The breakthrough came the day she realized the woman's children "rise up and call her blessed." Annie decided right then this woman must be older and probably postmenopausal. Annie said, "When my kids were young they didn't rise and call me blessed. They got up and called me to fix them some breakfast. When they are grown, *then* they'll call me 'blessed,' just as I do my own mother. By then I'll probably have the energy to take on some challenges I couldn't during the early years of child-rearing."

Christian men and women have tough choices to make about the priority of their marriage. In light of the obstacles confronting us, Annie and I use two simple ideas to help us keep our life together at the top of our list.

First, we cut out junk activities. You've heard of junk food? Well, junk activities are the ones that don't fit with what we have to have for a healthy marriage. What are we doing that might not really need to be done? Is it *urgent* that the house be spotless seven days a week? Do both cars *have* to be washed and waxed every Saturday? Sure these things may be important, but are they important enough to rob our families of good times together?

Even worthy activities can become junk if they duplicate other things we're already doing. After all, we can get sick by eating too much perfectly nutritious foods. So here's one very important question we use to evaluate our use of time: *What are we doing that others could do if we didn't?* For example, is there no one else who can sit in on all those church committee meetings if we withdrew? Will the world be worse off if we quit volunteering for some civic organizations?

Second, we try to limit junk expenditures. One of the greatest pressures that invade our family life comes in the push to have a paycheck that covers the lifestyle we *want* to lead. There are two ways to increase income effectiveness: work more or spend less. We try hard to keep our expenses down so we can spend more time together.

If the Lord has enabled you to provide an abundance of things without taking away from the priority of your marriage, that's great. I'm not trying to make you feel guilty. But as we've heard from many couples across America, "Today we have so much to do that we don't have any time to spend together."

Your family needs your *presence* much more than they need your *presents*. And your spouse needs more from you than just someone to help with the kids or bring in money. He or she needs you to be a *companion* and *friend* and *lover*—just like you were before the kids came along!

That Way Again

I want to feel love again
Just like I did way back when
We realized we were more than friends
I want to feel love like that again

I want to hear our old song again
Just like I did way back then
Oh, how we'd sway while that record would spin
I want to hear our old song again

If love has faded, the fault is mine
I once could see, but now I'm blind
I was the one who hid the view
Oh, Christ who heals, I come to You

I want to see that smile again
The one that told me way back then
My only love has just walked in
I want to see that smile again [2]

2

Feels like Love

by Steve

Ah, romance! I remember the passionate sighs, the $400 long-distance telephone bills, and sending roses for no reason except love. And how could I ever forget the feeling that life began the day *she* walked into my dreary existence. Yes, I do indeed remember when those emotions first began to churn in me for my Annie. I sent her chocolates, told her she was beautiful, and even came to a complete stop at all the stop signs when she rode with me. Romance was bustin' out all over, and it was grand. I was determined to do whatever it took to make this woman mine.

What I Did for Love

This woman of my dreams was born a country girl. And not just one of those "why don't you stand next to the tractor for the camera, honey" kind of country girls you see on television. Annie grew up on a dairy farm "up a holler" off a road called "Nine Mile Creek," in Mason County, West Virginia. In comparison, I was a city slicker. I was from Point Pleasant, in the same county, population 3000.

I was intent on doing whatever it took to impress this beautiful girl, and her family too. I figured I might as well start with her

farmer father. It didn't take many weekend visits to their farm to figure out that keeping the cows milked took up everyone's concen-
tration night and day, 365 days a year. *That's it!* I thought. *I'll get
out to the barn and help with the milking.* I was sure that Annie's dad
and the rest of her family would love me forever. So I looked for my
chance to help with the chores. That chance came one evening when
I went to pick Annie up for a date and learned from her mother that
she was out helping her dad with the milking.

Now bear in mind that Annie had been at this farm stuff a lot
longer than I had. When I stepped into the barn, there was my deli-
cate beloved slipping between those pungent, 700-pound cows. She
had a 10-penny nail in her hand and was poking and pushing them
around with the skill of a seasoned cowpuncher in the middle of
a roundup. How she managed while avoiding those piles of stuff
the cows had so carelessly deposited on the floor was beyond me. I
found out from Annie that they were about halfway finished with
the milking. I concluded I'd better be quick in finding something I
could do to help.

Then I found it! Over in the corner sat a steaming bucket of
water with a rag in it. Once before I'd seen Annie's dad using the
rag to wipe off the cows' udders. I assumed he was washing off the
"spigots" before he hooked the milking machine onto them. And it
looked like they were in need of a good cleaning to me. At last! A
job I could do without the danger of stepping too deep into cow-
doo. So I grabbed the bucket and headed for the milk-house sink
for a refill of clean water. I never expected to be nominated for sec-
retary of agriculture, but I did know a thing or two about cleaning.
I knew, for instance, that if warm water cleans well, hot water cleans
twice as good. So I turned on the faucet and let the water run over
one hand until it was way too hot to touch. I figured cows have thick
hides, so the hotter the better. I filled the bucket. With a smug grin,
I plunked the steaming bucket down next to Ol' Number 32. (All
the cows had ear tags with their numbers on them so you could tell

which one was which.) I gave 32 a nudge with my shoulder and said confidently, "You're next, sweetheart."

When I pulled the rag from the bucket, it was so hot I could hardly hold it. But what did a little pain matter? If a little suffering would win the favor of my future father-in-law and impress Annie, then suffer I would. So I wrung out that blister-producing rag a little and slapped it underneath and right on Ol' 32's tender parts.

That's when the lights went out. That angry Jersey Girl bucked in protest and sent me flying to the wall. As I peeled myself off the cinder blocks where I'd been thrown, Annie's dad quickly ran over to check out the commotion. He looked at me for a moment before shaking his head. He told me how impressed he was with my effort but added with a kindhearted smile that I didn't ever need to come back at milking time again.

What I hadn't known was that on a cold, West Virginia morning, those bovine milk faucets needed help "letting go" of their milk. A little *massage* with a *warm* rag stimulated the flow. Of course, the story of my tangle with cow #32 made its rounds through the family, and to this day they still affectionately refer to it as "the time Steve tried to sterilize the dairy herd."

I'll bet you have a story or two of your own about a few "udderly" ridiculous things romance drove you to do. If only this delicious state of emotional insanity was as easy to maintain as it was to fall into.

We Get in Trouble (When We Kiss)

We were both late for work again this morning
We nearly left on time; you know we tried
I almost lost my job; you got a warning
Guess we ought to shake hands
when we say goodbye 'cause

We get in trouble when we kiss
We get in trouble when we kiss like this
There ought to be a law against our lips
We get in trouble when we kiss

I flew in; you met me at the curb
I climbed inside the car; we kissed hello
That whistle was the next thing that we heard
And Barney Fife was screamin'
"You love birds are holding up the show!"

We get in trouble when we kiss
We get in trouble when we kiss like this
There ought to be a law against our lips
We get in trouble when we kiss

My Uncle Jack got sick and then he died
We were sittin' in the service that they had
Everything was going all right
'Til you just had to kiss me 'cause I was feeling so sad

We get in trouble when we kiss
We get in trouble when we kiss like this
There ought to be a law against our lips
We get in trouble when we kiss [1]

Secrets Hallmark Never Told You

Imagine this scene. An engaged couple strolls down the street, hand in hand, as pretty as a greeting card picture. Accidentally, the little lady steps on her man's foot. As she pulls her spike heel out of his arch, he gushes, "Don't worry about it, sweetheart. I've got a second foot right over here. Think nothing of it." Is he offended? Never! He seizes the opportunity to show her how much he adores her *and* how incredibly tough he is in the face of pain.

Now let's fast-forward to their fifth wedding anniversary. They're walking down the same street, still hand in hand. She's wearing those same shoes. Without warning she plants that spike into the hole in his foot she'd bored years before. But this time as she pulls the heel out, he gives her a look that would smack King Kong into submission. His words are not "Don't worry about it, baby!" Instead he barks, "Just because you look like Bigfoot doesn't mean you have to walk like him too! Why don'tcha watch where you're goin'?"

And he isn't the only one who's lost the romance. As far as he's concerned, when he asked her, "Wilt thou…?" five years earlier, she wilted and hasn't revived since.

Unfortunately, in far too many cases romance seems to be a pre-marital condition that is cured instantly by a trip to the altar. A woman in one of our marriage conferences once gave this definition of romance: "It's the attraction during courtship that vanishes with the words 'I do.'" Too many husbands and wives take "I do" to mean "Maybe I *did* when I was still trying to woo you, but I sure *don't* intend to anymore!"

One young man we met at a marriage seminar wrote, "Romance comes from walking hand in hand on a moonlit beach with the wind blowing lightly in our faces—and our walk leading us back to our cottage where there awaits a fire, roses, and satin sheets whispering our names." His wife smiled and added, "And I'll be looking for a nice, new piece of jewelry on that satin pillow."

This couple's idea of what it takes to make the sweet pie of exciting love sounds great, but are these really the essential ingredients to stir romance? If they are, what happens the next morning when the twosome fusses over little things, such as who is going to clean out the ashes from the fireplace or whose job it is to water the drooping, store-bought roses?

If God wants marriage to be a picture to the world of Christ's eternal romance with His bride, the church, then some questions arise (Ephesians 5). Does the passionate partnership He wants for a husband and wife always require crackling fires, fresh roses, satin sheets, and fancy jewelry? If so, how can we possibly keep it alive in the harsh daylight when it comes time to pay the bills for the rented cottage and expensive jewelry?

So, where does true and lasting romance come from, anyway?

A "Gimme" Point of View

The fire of romance that keeps greeting card companies up and running is stoked by the fuel of "gimme." In other words, a man can be attracted to a particular woman because of what she has to offer him. Maybe he believes he'll finally feel important if someone as beautiful as she is will love *him*. Perhaps it's her warmth or when she compliments him the feeling of worth he feels. Possibly her willingness to follow him anywhere gives him a sense of power or control. Or maybe her readiness to lead him makes him feel secure. He may see winning her love as his chance to capture a lifetime supply of the companionship, the lovemaking, or the encouragement he longs for. Whatever the reason, he wants her for what she can do for him. These qualities in her make him want to give himself to win her. That's when the romance rockets explode across the sky.

Of course, there's a catch to this dynamic. If a man marries a woman because he wanted a 38-24-38 knockout to parade before his friends, what happens when three pregnancies have changed the curves of her figure? He stops giving to her or he starts criticizing her. And when that happens, things go downhill.

And if a woman is attracted to a man because of his pursuit—the cards, candy, kind comments, and his undivided attention—what happens if he fails to consistently do that? And what happens if the strong leadership she was promised during their courtship begins to look more like domineering bossiness? She quits giving, and the fires of romance in her heart start to die down.

Where Is True Romance?

Thankfully, there's an answer to the question of where *true* romance within marriage is found. It's not in what we can *get* from one another, it's in what we can *give* to one another. A "serve you" type of love produces acts of giving that stir up the kind of romance that endures the decades and satisfies our deepest cravings for love. And the love grows whether great waves of mushy feeling come washing in with it or not.

The passion that arcs between Christ and His church has less to do with emotion than it does with a mutual decision to give ourselves in service to each other. Jesus explained to His disciples, "The Son of Man did not come to be served, but to serve" (Mark 10:45). Lasting romance begins when a husband and wife view their marriage as continual opportunities to meet each other's needs. This love springs from hearts that are grateful for Christ's lavish, love-generated service to us. Though serving each other often results in the kind of electricity Hallmark would call romantic, it will continue to survive even when the rushing tides of emotion have ebbed.

Before Annie and I were married, a wise friend passed on this piece of advice: "Steve, let all that you do and say be a service to her. Pleasing *her* should be your highest priority after serving God. Put her concerns above your own. If you do this, you'll be blessed with a relationship that is not only full of joy, but also most pleasing to the Lord." What my friend was accurately describing is based on a passage found in the New Testament:

> If you have any encouragement from being united with Christ, if any comfort from his love, if any common sharing in the Spirit, if any tenderness and compassion, then make my joy complete by being like-minded, having the same love, being one in spirit and of one mind. Do nothing out of selfish ambition or vain conceit. Rather, in humility value others above yourselves, not looking to your own interests but each of you to the interests of others (Philippians 2:1-4 NIV).

To be honest, I've not found my friend's advice or that passage in Philippines the easiest to follow. But I do agree that as I've chosen to focus on Annie's needs, a servant's heart *in action* does generate romance at its best.

Maybe your marriage started on the wrong foot, like the man I heard about who pleaded with his girlfriend, "Let's get married. I'm tired of being charming!" Even with a beginning as bad as that, your spouse and you can find yourselves enjoying the same freshness, love, respect, and sense of adventure you did as newlyweds, whether 5, 10, 20, or 30 years have passed. How? By learning new ways to care for each other, listening to each other more intently, and meeting each other's changing needs. Romance doesn't have to wither. As a servant's "giving heart" replaces the "gimme heart," your marriage will blossom and grow anew.

How Do You Get a Servant's Heart?

The responsibilities and demands of daily life have a way of taking the steam of romance out of spouses. Many men I know come home from a hard day at work and just want to relax. Because we feel as if we've been jumping all day to the demands of our bosses, customers, and fellow workers, we naturally feel like we'd rather be left *alone*. So when we get home, we want to do just that, often forgetting that a woman's reaction to her tough day (or even a great day) is to want to share it with the man she loves. Who is going to make up the difference when this gap opens up between husband and wife?

Annie and I aren't marriage counselors, psychologists, professional counselors, or ministers. We are, however, very happily married and have been for nearly 40 years. In the middle of a world where more than half the couples marrying will later decide to split up, we're still together and growing closer and stronger as a couple. We face the same money pressures, job struggles, and parenting hassles as others do, but we've discovered how to press on and find joy (most of the time) in the journey. Besides those things mentioned that can challenge the quality of romance we like to enjoy, there's one that deserves a special note because I'm sure you can relate to it. It's the challenge of dealing with the stark differences between man and woman.

To help us deal with our various differences, Annie and I sat down and listed all we could think of. Here's a *partial* list of what we came up with that I turned into a song Annie and I sing at concerts and when we conduct marriage seminars:

Incompatibility

Steve: "I like a little mayo"
Annie: "Mustard is my thing"
Steve: "Make my bread as white as cotton"
Annie: "I'll have wheat with seven grains"

Annie: "And a little candle glowing when we eat
is what I like"
Steve: "I need to see what I'm consuming,
so please turn on the lights"

Annie: "I go to bed before the news"
Steve: "I'm still awake at two AM"
Annie: "I'm up before the chickens"
Steve: "If I can, I'm sleeping in"

Steve: "I like wearing huntin' clothes"
Annie: "I like huntin' clothes to wear"
Annie: "I'll always ask directions"
Steve: "I'll find my own way there"

Together: We've got incompatibility everywhere we turn
But still we stay together 'cause there's
a lesson we have learned
That if this man and woman were in
every way the same
One of us would not be needed,
and wouldn't that be a shame

Annie: "I like a walk in the park"
Steve: "And I would rather run"
Steve: "How far can we go on empty"
Annie: "I've never seen as fun"

Steve: "I like talking to my buddies
when we're teeing off at ten"
Annie: "My greens and conversation are
a salad bar with friends"

Annie: "My feet are like December"
Steve: "And mine are like July"
Annie: "While I'm piling on the blankets"
Steve: "I lay there and fry"

Annie: "I married Ebenezer Scrooge"
Steve: "I married Mrs. Claus"
Annie: "While I'm watching *Casablanca*"
Steve: "I'd rather be watching football"

Together: We've got incompatibility everywhere we turn
But still we stay together 'cause there's
a lesson we have learned
That if this man and woman were in
every way the same
One of us would not be needed,
and wouldn't that be a shame [2]

While Annie and I could have allowed our differences to divide us, thankfully we've found that we can disagree about things without married life becoming difficult. Today we consider the "oppositeness" in us to be like spice in chili. Without the spice, the dish would be bland and tasteless. How did we arrive at this conclusion? By enlisting the wisdom in Philippians 2 and putting the other person's concerns above our individual ones. This principle works in all areas of marriage, but especially in the romance department.

We want to help you find this kind of fulfilling romance in your journey together, the kind we've found in ours through serving one another. And what has been our guide to making serving work for us? It's certainly not the world around us, where marriage is continually made sport of, such as these bumper stickers: "It used to be wine, woman and song. Now it's beer, the old lady, and television" and "Friends don't let friends get married."

We're not simply drawing on the examples of other Christian couples either, as valuable as their models of romance can be. Ultimately, it's not *what* has been our guide to true romance, it's *Who*. The expert we've consulted is available 'round the clock, understands us better than we do, has the most wisdom, and wants to involve Himself totally with us—all without making us feel foolish or guilty. You've probably guessed we're talking about Jesus.

Jesus doesn't expect us to pour out love from an empty bucket. He wants to fill our lives with His love, and from that fullness we are able to give freely. When Christ wanted to set a powerful example of service to His disciples, He drew on God's resources. The Scripture says:

> Jesus, knowing that the Father had given all things into His hands, and that He had come forth from God and was going back to God, got up from supper, and laid aside His garments; and taking a towel, He girded Himself. Then He poured water into the basin, and began to wash the disciples' feet and to wipe them with the towel (John 13:3-5).

Jesus' human needs were met by God; therefore, He could give unselfishly. As we look to Him to meet our needs, we will have all we require, including the love we need to joyfully serve our spouses.

It doesn't take much to acquire a servant's heart, really. First, we simply have to admit our need. Christ came to serve the sinner, not those who consider themselves righteous (Mark 2:17). We aren't eligible to receive His work in our hearts until we admit our sinfulness, including our selfishness and our inability to change ourselves into the givers we want to be.

Maybe you're not sure what a servant's heart looks like because you've never seen one in action. Perhaps your parents weren't the best examples of what it means to love with selfless devotion. If that's the case, you still have a great role model. The greatest servant of all, Jesus, is your perfect example. He served even as He resisted temptation and lived a sinless life. He served even as He allowed Himself to be brutally nailed to a cross so He could redeem humanity. And now He serves you in heaven by interceding for you with your heavenly Father. Jesus shows you how to serve, and then He empowers you to do it. All you need to do is ask for His help.

If you admit your need and ask God to do surgery on your selfishness, you can expect Him to say yes. He's promised to never turn away those who seek Him. Then you can commit yourself to serve your spouse in *God's* strength. He will commit to helping you do that too. You've chosen to align yourself with the design of heaven when you decide to love by giving, so heaven will align itself with you. God may reward your efforts by changing your mate in ways that please you. Or He may change *you* instead. Or He might do both. In any case, you'll come out ahead because when you give for Jesus' sake and in His name, He guarantees you will receive.

No matter how good—or bad—your marriage is today, you can begin at once to change it for the better by deciding to serve your spouse as much as possible. If you could use another good example of a couple who has the "servant's heart" attitude going for them, take note of the husband and wife in the following lyric. Their willingness to see the other's needs as more important than his or her own (not that our individual needs aren't important) provides them with rich soil where true romance can grow.

Feels like Love

He knew all along it was one of her dreams
So he put some George Strait in the music machine
Then he took her hand and said, "You know I can't dance
But darling just for you, I'm gonna take that chance"

And she said, "Ooh, baby, I can't believe it's true
I never thought I'd be dancin' with you
Ooh, baby, thank you so much
Might look like dancin', but it feels like love!"

And now it's Sunday in the afternoon
She knows what he's doing in the TV room
Watching cars go round in circles ain't her cup of tea
But she says, "Turn it up; scoot over, darlin';
make some room for me"

And he says, "Ooh, baby, I can't believe it's true
I never thought I'd watch racin' with you
Ooh, baby, thank you so much
Might look like racin', but it feels like love!"

Now she smiles when he says,
"Baby, won't you come and dance with me"
And he smiles when they're sittin' in the stands
down in Bristol, TN…
and they're both wearing number three

He says, "Ooh, baby, I can't believe it's true
I never thought I'd watch racin' with you
Ooh, baby, thank you so much
Might look like racin', but it feels like love"
She says, "Might look like dancin', but it feels like love" [3]

Working Together

by Annie

When we got married, most of the Christian marriage formulas boiled down to one easy transaction: Man in charge + Woman who submits = Uninterrupted bliss. If you took this teaching to its extreme (which, sadly, *I* always seem to do with any good teaching), you might believe that a wife needs to have only two words in her vocabulary: "Yes, dear." I was young and eager to please the Lord and my new husband, so I determined to "yes, dear" my way to happiness. For instance, when we'd get ready for an evening out, Steve would ask, "Where do you want to go?"

"Oh, anywhere *you* want to go, dear," I'd reply.

"Is there any special kind of food you are hungry for?" he'd ask.

"Oh, anything *you* want to eat, dear."

"Which of these two movies sounds better to you?"

"Whichever one *you'd* like to see, dear."

All right. I wasn't quite *that* bad, but you get the idea. This caricature of mindless submission I'd adopted is what led Steve and me to what we call the "Copperhead Confrontation." In the days before our garage apartment (and if you had one of those, you'll remember it was the one without a washer and dryer!), we shared a farmhouse with two other couples. Be assured that we weren't doing this out of a great love for communal living. The farmhouse rent was $100 a month, and only by splitting the rent three ways could we make the payment. (It took a lot less money to live, but money was hard to come by back in the "old" days.)

If the idea of farm living felt comfortable and romantic to me at the start, all the romance faded the day I found a snake in the yard. And *that* was the good news! The bad news was that the snake was a poisonous and potentially deadly copperhead. And where there was one, there was bound to be more.

Of course, I yelled for Steve. He and his friend Ron came running. They went after that snake while I stayed on the porch and cheered for the great hunters stalking their prey. Well, the snake was smarter than they were, and it eluded them at every turn. Then I saw it coming right toward *me*! I looked down and saw that I was standing right over a small hole in the porch floor. Instantly, I realized the snake had taken up residence there and was headed back home. (Fortunately, it hadn't occurred to me yet that a whole pack of its nasty relatives might be right under my feet or I would have gone hysterical.) The snake, meantime, was quickly slithering toward its hole in the porch. Steve, realizing the snake was about to get away yelled to me, "Grab that snake!"

Any sane woman would have burst out laughing at such a ridiculous idea and, instead, taken a flying leap *off* the porch. But not me. At the sound of my "master's" voice, all those months of training myself seized control of my faculties. Basically, my mental reaction was "Tarzan say, 'Grab snake,' Me grab snake." And just as the copperhead started into the hole, I reached down and clamped onto him. He stiffened in my hand. I suddenly realized what I'd done, screamed, jerked back my arm and hand, and let go, sending the creature flying into the yard. Steve and Ron promptly did him in.

Steve came stomping over, the color drained from his face. (He wasn't the only one!) "Annie! I can't believe you grabbed that snake!" he said, wide-eyed.

"I can't believe you *asked* me to!" I choked out angrily.

That was the day we both decided we needed some balance in the way we came to our decisions. We weren't sure what the Lord wanted when He called for submission in marriage, but we knew it couldn't be this. As we studied the Scripture, we realized we'd overlooked an important truth. God called us fellow heirs of the grace of life (1 Peter 3:7). He sees us as teammates—two people sharing a yoke just like a team of oxen do. We are to pull *together* to get the job done. For a yoke of oxen to be effective, both have to be pulling part of the load. All this time I'd been asking Steve to carry the whole load while I sat back passively and enjoyed the ride. Except, of course, when I automatically accepted strange orders like "Grab that snake!"

Now, a yoke of oxen only work well if they're headed the same direction. In our "do your own thing" age, this kind of teamwork is especially hard to pull off. Every television sitcom, magazine, and talk show tries to convince us we've got to watch out for number one. They tell us that a strong, happy person is one who holds tightly to independence, lest he or she be taken advantage of. How different this is from the teamwork model of New Testament marriage, where each partner seeks to "submit to one another out of reverence for Christ" (Ephesians 5:21 NIV).

Christians marry not just so each person will be happier, or less lonely, or more understood, though those benefits will surely be true of a marriage centered in God. Marriage was designed to honor God, so our fear of the Lord and our reverence for Him motivates us to work as a team for His glory.

Sometimes working as a team means I must give up the way I want to do things. Sometimes it means dialoguing until my ideas fit together with my spouse's. Other times it means taking charge. It's like the time Steve got an ear infection and refused to see the doctor. Now, when I say he had an infection, I'm understating the situation. He was so sick that his eardrums burst, and he was bleeding from both ears. There he was, writhing in pain, but the man absolutely refused to see a doctor. I listened to his moaning as long as I could. When I could stand it no longer, I called a specialist and explained his symptoms. The doctor agreed it was serious and said, "It's closing time, but if you tell him to come in right now, I'll wait." Unfortunately, this medical confirmation failed to overcome my husband's physician phobia. Steve made no move to budge from his bed. I knew the time had come for drastic measures.

"Steve," I announced, "in First Corinthians it says a wife has rights over her husband's body. So those ears may be on your head, but they are *my* ears too. And I'm taking *my* ears to the doctor. You can go with clothes or without clothes, I don't care. But *my* ears are getting medical treatment!"

I reached down to pull him out of bed. Steve was worse than a child. I could have carried a child to the car, but this 175-pounder, no way. So I prodded him out from under the covers.

He saw there'd be no dissuading me, so he grumpily staggered out of bed, fumbled his way into a warm-up suit, and let me drag him to the doctor.

In the car on the way back home, I apologized for being so bossy.

When he forgave me, he also acknowledged I'd helped him do what he knew he ought to do anyway. We drove home in peace. (By the way, "our" ears recovered completely.)

If authority is a shared effort, what about the practical, everyday management of the home and family? Some people believe the wife should be responsible for child-rearing and housework, while the husband should be the sole financial provider and the bearer of the heavier household tasks, especially outside maintenance. Wouldn't it be nice if life were just that simple? If there weren't so many gray areas?

How should the tasks be divided in a marriage? We decided that it depends on what's best for the team effort to honor the Lord and on how we can best serve each other. With us, for example, Steve pays the monthly bills on a regular basis. We do it this way because I tend to operate in a general, idea-oriented mode, while Steve thinks more precisely. Generalities have their place, but balancing a checkbook isn't one of them. So to maintain our financial solvency, we agreed the bill-paying would be best done by Steve.

When we purchased a different home, I did the final negotiating with the Realtor because I thrive on negotiating and resolving conflicts. I find it exhilarating to offer and counter-offer until an agreement is reached, while that process makes Steve uncomfortable.

Should the husband or wife handle the business end of family life? We believe it depends on each one's skill set as well as needs. Sometimes a task may shift from one to the other. This happens when the one who is usually responsible for a certain job is under a particular pressure of some sort or simply needs help. For example, I normally do the grocery shopping, but if I'm overtaxed, Steve's been known to push a cart up and down the aisles. Likewise, I help him shoulder one of his usual tasks when circumstances are pressing in on him.

We really do believe in the trade-off system I just described, but because marriage is a union of two imperfect people, it doesn't always work out quite so smoothly. Sometimes the things we care about are hard to let go of. And each partner doesn't always have the same idea of what's best for the team or what's the best way to get the job accomplished. What then? This was the question plaguing the Chapman household one Christmas. When it comes to Christmas, Steve becomes Scrooge and I turn into Sister Claus. Hardly a workable combination!

You see, one of my dreams growing up was holding extravagant celebrations at Christmas. The holidays I longed for looked like a reenactment of an over-the-top Christmas special on TV. Picture a fire crackling, cookies baking, and an elegantly ornamented, beribboned home decked out with evergreen boughs. As I imagined this beautiful, festive display, I could see my family posed in a scene lovely enough to adorn a greeting card. We'd all be dressed to the teeth in velvet and plaid taffeta as we gathered around the piano to sing carols in four-part harmony.

Growing up, we didn't have anyone in the family who played the piano. And with six kids, we never did get the house *that* immaculate, let alone keep it that way long enough to belt out a chorus of "Hark, the Herald Angels Sing." And I've yet to see all eight members of my family in a good mood at the same time. So singing or no singing, we could never make such a holiday fantasy come true. So I tucked away my dream for the days when I'd have my own home and family. Surely then I'd be able to celebrate the way I'd always hoped.

Steve also brought his own convictions for celebrating Christmas. While I love everything about Christmas—the decorations, the singing, the hustle and bustle—the one-and-only thing Steve liked about it was the birth of our Savior, Jesus Christ. To Steve, all the rest of it needed to be thrown out with the used wrapping paper.

So what happens to the glory of a smooth-working Christian marriage when the wife is Santa's biggest fan and the husband says, "Shoot the reindeer and cook them for supper"? Our first attempt at a solution was to *compromise* in an attempt to keep peace. Steve tried to avoid conflict by bringing in and then letting me decorate a tree. I grudgingly agreed that was a real compromise because he worried that the whole idea of trees and ornaments was a pagan custom that probably shouldn't be part of a Christian celebration of the birth of the Savior. Steve also allowed me to buy gifts for the children, another tough compromise since he thought all this gift-giving taught them materialism and greed.

I tried to inject the season with what celebrating I could without offending him, but I felt sorry for myself the whole time. Okay, so we had a tree, but it never would have made it on a television Christmas special. The tree was a dreadful, aluminum thing I picked up at a garage sale. The box was marked $1, but the lady didn't put up any resistance when I offered half that amount. I'm sure you can guess how charming our tree was. To decorate it, I baked sugar cookies with paper-clip hangers embedded in one end. I figured buying ornaments would send my husband into an emotional tailspin. The kids did get gifts from us, but, at Steve's insistence, only one apiece. His argument was, "With one nice gift, they'll remember what they got!"

Both of us were trying to get what we could of our own way. And make no mistake—both of us were sure we were also doing what was best for the husband/wife team and for the family as a whole. Steve felt he needed to hold firm because he was saving our kids from worldliness. I believed we needed all this celebrating to make the birth of our Lord one of the high points of our year as a family. And both of us could have made a highly persuasive and even spiritual-sounding case for why we were right.

There was no open warfare, but our differing view of Christmas was *not* something we joked about with ourselves or others. Neither of us saw much that was funny in the other person's stubbornness. An uneasy truce reigned—until one snowy, Christmas morning. The kids had opened their one gift from us and then unwrapped the few others that family and compassionate neighbors had provided. When the last one had been ripped open, one of them looked up and asked, "Where's the rest of it?"

With that innocent question, Hurricane Steve unleashed his fury. He rose to his feet with holy fire blazin' in his eyes. He thundered into his favorite sermon on the evils of Christmastime. Eventually, he ran out of steam. I'm sure these kinds of sermons are more enjoyable to preach when you have an eager audience shouting "Amen" and "You tell 'em, brother." Steve received no such encouragement from his captive congregation of three. He stopped pacing and, still waving his finger in the air, returned to his chair to open *his* gifts. The rest of us retreated to our rooms.

Steve and I didn't talk for the rest of the day. I was hurt and angry, and my feelings grew as the day wore on. I felt I'd sacrificed major slabs of my holiday dream for this man. And instead of being appreciated, I'd gotten a lecture. I realized too that any hopes I still cherished for having a picture-pretty Christmas would have to die. Steve was *not* going to budge an inch on this issue.

Steve, meanwhile, was rumbling around with his own set of angry reactions. And that night we violated Scripture and let the sun go down on our wrath (Ephesians 4:26). I lay in bed crying while Steve had the gall to curl up next to me and go to sleep. But was he really asleep? I wasn't convinced. He made some half-baked attempts at fake snoring though. He even offered that "I'm falling into a deep sleep now" jerk. He didn't have to go that far. The word "jerk" was already going through my mind.

The next morning we got into the car for the full-day's trip to our parents' homes in West Virginia. As we drove there to "share the joy," Steve's and my anger were in full force. Neither of us was willing to take a step toward healing by yielding our wills to the Holy Spirit or even hammering out a compromise between us. Seven hours of frozen fury followed. It wasn't until we crossed the border of West Virginia, about 30 miles from our destination, that Steve broke the silence. He admitted later that his initiative wasn't motivated by great remorse but by the embarrassment he'd feel if his parents saw us acting like this.

"Annie, we have to have a conversation about our conflict."

From between clenched teeth I replied icily, "I'm listening."

Steve had a conversation about our conflict.

"I guess I've been a jerk about this whole Christmas thing," he began tentatively.

"I know you have." No thaw in sight.

"Do you think we can patch this riff between us so we can go to our parents' homes and have a nice Christmas?" he asked.

"The prospects of us having a nice Christmas are questionable," I returned, "but I'm willing to be civil to your family while we're visiting them."

This initial interchange could go down in our personal history as the worst example of loving cooperation. And we were pushed to it mostly by our pride. During the next two days we talked off and on about Christmas. We offered this solution and that, but each of them turned into a power struggle between us. Anger and hurt feelings made the issue of *who* would be right more important than *what* was right. It appeared we'd never find a middle ground.

So I decided to give in. "Steve," I said slowly, "for years I've tried hard to make Christmas special for our family, but I've failed. I'm giving you the freedom to make our Christmas into whatever you want. I won't push for anything or do anything at all about Christmas unless you ask me to."

I hope you can imagine what a difficult decision that was for me. Steve had proved himself unworthy of my trust when it came to Christmas, so entrusting him with *my* Christmas came as easily as handing one of my children over to a mad gorilla. I realized I could well be opening myself to spending the next Christmas in a cheerless, giftless (but totally unmaterialistic) "celebration." However, I also knew that insisting on getting my way had resulted in a serious division between Steve and me. And that was bringing dishonor to the Lord, who wanted our marriage to be an example of the way love and unity flow between Christ and His church (believers). I knew the Lord wanted me to give up my TV Christmas Special dream for His sake.

Even though Steve had disappointed me regarding this holiday, as I reviewed *all* I knew of him I realized anew that his Christmas "Scroogery" wasn't motivated by selfishness. He really was concerned for our family—even if we had different ideas about what was best for us. If he was wrong in this decision about how we would celebrate Christmas, so what? I thought, *Steve is not stingy for 364 days a year. Why let one day out of a year ruin our life together? Why let it negatively impact our children?* While I desperately loved Christmas, I decided I loved God and the man He'd given me more.

From that point on, the next Christmas holiday was in the hands of Steve Chapman. And because I trusted that Steve Chapman was in the hands of the Lord, I was at peace. And interestingly, without giving me one clue, the Lord was already doing some work in Steve. Not long before Christmastime, Steve attended a men's conference where the speaker taught from Malachi 2 and talked about the terrible consequences of wounding your wife's spirit. Such an act, the speaker emphasized, could cut off a man's communication with God (Malachi 2:13-14; 1 Peter 3:7).

Steve realized that the tremendous disappointment I expressed about our holiday was really an outpouring of a wounded spirit. He told me later it stirred the fear of God in his heart. If shielding our kids from the awakening of greed resulted in wounding his wife, he knew it couldn't be right before God. When I told him I was going to trust him to make the right decision about our next Christmas holiday, he knew the power struggle between us had dissolved so he felt free to consider what might be best for *all* of us.

When December arrived, I stuck to my commitment to leave celebrating Christmas up to Steve. Since he made no requests of me, I didn't do any shopping or decorating. Our halls may not have been decked with boughs of holly (in our case, boughs of tacky aluminum), but the tension we'd felt before wasn't there either.

Then one evening, Steve and the kids pulled on hats, coats, and boots and trooped out to the car without inviting me along. I busied myself with cleaning up the kitchen and paid little attention, figuring it was just a father, son, and daughter outing. When they returned a couple hours later, Steve called to me from outside the front door. "Annie, will you come here a minute?"

When I opened the door, there he stood holding a *real* Christmas tree. The children stood by his side practically glowing. I stepped out of the way as they carried in boxes of decorations, lights, a centerpiece for the table, candles, and even a recording of Christmas carols. We put on the music and decorated that beautiful, fragrant tree.

Steve made a fire, and I started a batch of cookies. It was a delightful scene that completely fulfilled my Christmas dreams. And it's been repeated every year since.

I don't want you to get the idea that my man did a total turnaround. He still insists on holding up the decorations and asking the Lord to "sanctify these pagan items" before we put them on the tree—half out of conviction now, I think, and half out of orneriness. And the children still only get one gift from us. But Steve and I shop for Christmas together now. I no longer sneak around trying to do Christmas my way, and Steve no longer sits back sulking and wanting Christmas done his way. Because we each chose to give to the other out of reverence for Christ, this time of rejoicing in our Lord's birth is the genuine celebration God intended.

Real Submission

What was important to us were the lessons we learned. True submission starts with each person's submission to Christ. Marital decisions aren't a seesaw, with the husband at one end and the wife at the other. There is always a third, overriding will to consider. What does the Lord want done here? We have to first submit to Him, listen to Him, and then act on what He says. Thus, there's no struggle except to find what He wants. After years of marriage, Steve and I have learned to be grateful for anything that forces us to work out the hard stuff because it draws us closer together.

We all come into our marriages with expectations. Some we're aware of; some we're not. If communication and compromise result in these expectations being met, that's wonderful. In most cases that is likely to happen. But sometimes deferring to each other costs a great deal. I know my Christmas dream may be a small situation compared to those you may hold dear, but when we choose to submit (defer) to our partners out of reverence for *Christ*, we are doing it as an act of giving, of worshipping our Savior, not because we expect something back from our mates.

Sometimes when we give our dreams to God, He gives it back completely, just as He did with my holiday desires. Other times, He may change us so that our desires aren't as important to us as they once were. And still other times He may enable us to receive more of Him—His peace, His grace, His power in the situation. That's the richest return of all! God is no one's debtor, and when we give to Him through deferring to our partners, He promises He will give back to us in greater measure than we gave.

So Who Is the Real Boss?

The question of who will be the boss in a marriage partnership can turn every minor decision into a major struggle for control. But Christ is the boss of our married life (and our individual lives). When we honor Him and walk with Him by serving and giving to our spouses, He'll improve the state of our unions.

By the way, the work of the Holy Spirit was further evidenced when Steve embraced the "Christmas Spirit" even more and we recorded a Christmas CD. In fact, he wrote some of the songs for that production, including this one I'm sure you'll enjoy.

The Stable

Joseph had the money; it's not 'cause he was poor
Still he and Mary were turned away at the innkeeper's door
And I have often wondered why the Father wanted it this way
But there's a message in the place where Christ was born
Spoken in the kindest way

My heart is like that stable
It was dark and cold and unclean
And though it was unworthy
It was chosen for the presence of the King

Like the shepherds came to find Him
There are those who seek Him now
And in a place so unsuspecting
The Savior of the world can be found

In hearts that are like that stable
They're dark and cold and unclean
And though they are unworthy
They are chosen for the presence of the King[1]

Excess Baggage

by Annie

*H*i. My name is Annie, and I am a Packaholic." If there were an organization for compulsive overpackers—that is, people who must pack everything they own in a suitcase each time they travel no matter how long they'll be away—I'd be their Woman of the Year. I know, I know. Any person who has traveled full-time with a family of four *should* have packing down to an exact science. I certainly should have learned by now how to fit a month's worth of clothes into two carry-ons and a guitar case. However, that's simply not how it is.

It's not that I don't try. I make lists, coordinate outfits, and thrash myself mentally for all the things we took the last time and wound up not needing. But when it comes time to actually stuff the suitcases, all my careful control goes *ka-plooey*. In go the extra purses and matching pairs of shoes, not to mention a complete assortment of clothing alternatives in case we hit cold weather, or hot weather, or rain, or a formal affair, or a casual get-together. On and on it goes. And this is true even if it's just for a weekend.

Admittedly, with the flying regulations now imposed by the airlines, I've had to make some major adjustments in how much luggage I can take with me. However, when we have the luxury of traveling by ground, my old habits kick into high gear and the back of the van gets filled to the ceiling.

It's possible to come into marriage with excess baggage as well. And I'm not talking about Samsonite suitcases. The baggage burdening us may be wounds from the past—hurts and painful memories that keep us bound up and hinder or stop our ability to grow with our mates on the journey toward greater marital intimacy.

Steve and I hear of these wounds continually as we minister to people at concerts, seminars, and other events. Often we receive letters from men and women all across the country who suffer deeply from the scars of a painful past. If you're plagued by these scars, you may find some of their stories hard to take. Sometimes just admitting you *have* wounds can cause great pain; yet it is vital to your spiritual and emotional growth that you identify these hurts and give them to Jesus. Without His healing, the weight of this excess baggage will squash your joy and wreak havoc on your capacity to love and be loved.

The Baggage of Abuse

One young woman from Texas shared this painful story:

> When I was a child, there were many nights that I would lie awake wondering [how long it would be before] the lights came on. And then I'd hear my mother yell, "Harold, stop hitting me!" And I'd lie in bed with tears in my eyes, waiting for the moment when my mother would come rushing into the bedroom to hurry all us children out of bed to flee from daddy.

Another woman wrote:

> I come from a home of two alcoholic parents [and] five children, of whom I'm the oldest. There was every abuse you can imagine in our home…I have discovered during

the last few years that all three of my brothers were being abused by my mother and that they, like my sister and I, were so caught up in what we thought was OUR fault that we didn't tell anyone.

The abuse statistics are mind-boggling and horrendous. One out of every three girls and one out of every six boys will be sexually molested by the time they reach age 18. And it isn't just children who are forced to carry the baggage of abuse. You may be a wife or husband who has suffered the agony of physical or emotional battering from your marriage partner. The website www.sistercare.com reports that one out of two women is battered at some time in her life. Approximately 4000 women die each year due to domestic violence. And reports of husbands being abused by their wives have been increasing. Abuses are occurring at the same rate to people regardless of income level and religious belief. In her book *Conjugal Crime*, Terry Davison tells of growing up in a home where her father beat her mother. And he was serving as a Christian minister at the time! At church he spoke respectfully of the things of God, but at home he behaved brutally, sometimes spewing out verbal or physical abuse just before or after saying grace at the table. A woman in just such a situation wrote to us:

> My marriage is in terrible trouble. I am a Christian and so is my husband, even though you would never know it by his actions right now. My husband degrades me constantly and verbally abuses me in many ways. He tells me all the problems that we have are all my fault. I am trying to serve the Lord and keep the family together, but it's really hard. I realize that [when] marriages fall apart, the children are the broken pieces, and I don't want my children to be broken pieces. I don't know how much more I can stand.

Abuse is not the only baggage that can weigh us down, of course.

The Baggage of Neglect

God intended for us to see His loving care illustrated in our family of origin. Steve, for instance, has many wonderful memories of his father. I'll let him share with you:

> I clearly recall the times my father would drive our family through the hills of West Virginia. I'd be standing right behind him in the car (this was before seat belt laws) with my chin planted on Dad's shoulder. I recall how he would glimpse at me in the rearview mirror. I was seven years old, awkward and sickly looking. My teeth went in all directions, and a serious illness had left me with a skinny body and dark circles under my eyes. My dad could probably see he'd never be able to sit on the bleachers and cheer as his boy blasted 50 yards for a touchdown.
>
> Even knowing full-well what his son might never be, he'd still say to me, "Steve, let's you and me talk." He'd take one hand off the steering wheel, reach back, and gently pat the back of my head. And we'd talk—about everything and nothing.

Now that's what God intended parents to do for their children. But it may not have been what you experienced in your home. As one young woman wrote:

> My father took very little interest in my life as I was growing up. Because of the business my parents were in, they had no time for me or for a normal family life. They did the best they could, but I grew up feeling terribly insecure.
>
> When I was about 12 years old I began being noticed by boys. By my mid-teens, I was involved with men much older than I was. It seemed I was always looking for men who looked like my dad.

I married young, after having become involved with a man physically. I felt so guilty and knew what I was doing was wrong. Two children later we divorced. I know now I was just looking for my daddy's love.

The Baggage of Anger

Not all emotional baggage is from actions or events that happened to us directly. One young parent wrote:

> I am a single parent. My husband informed me that what he wanted to do in life did not include a wife and kids. So since the summer of 1986, the kids and I have been on our own. I have two great kids—a girl and a boy, ages 6 and 5. I am sure the divorce has really affected both of them...

This woman went on to say that she didn't know how to get free of the gnawing anger at her husband for what he'd done to their kids. Daily she lived with the pain and loss she saw on their faces.

The Baggage of Broken Relationships

Broken friendships can also load you down so that all your other relationships are negatively affected. An employee confided with us in a letter:

> Two people whom I work with and trust deeply hurt me in a way I don't know how to explain. They betrayed me. I felt so rejected that I kept getting more and more depressed until I actually tried to commit suicide.

Or the breakdown may be between you and your spouse. A wife wrote:

> My husband and I are now separated; we were married for nearly 20 years. He says he loves me, but I don't know

if I can trust him. We are separated because he wants to go out with other women.

He says he is sorry and that he wants us to have another chance. I don't know if I can go through all this again. This has happened before. I have left him a number of times. I don't know why, but I still love him. Do you believe marriages are made in heaven? I used to think ours was till all these troubles came. I just don't know if we can have trust again.

And it isn't just women who know this kind of heartbreak. A husband sent this plea:

Will you please pray for me and my family? My wife and I married nearly 20 years ago. We divorced last year but remarried 6 months later. Now we're headed for the divorce courts again. We have four beautiful children and my heart is aching.

My parents divorced as I was going into adolescence. At that time pornography got a hook in my jaw. Even though I received Christ as my Savior at age 18 (largely through my wife's influence), the roots of this sin were not dealt with. We felt a call to the ministry, went to Bible college, served in the pastorate for 10 years and also worked in other Christian services. All this time I lived with guilt and a sense of hypocrisy due to period-ically, yet regularly, yielding to this insatiable lust of the flesh. As one thing led to another, I eventually became unfaithful physically as well as mentally. When my wife learned of it she was destroyed.

The last 5 years have been unbelievable. To make a long story short, she is emotionally dead toward me today, and says she doesn't want to try to make our marriage work anymore. I feel totally responsible.

The Baggage of Wrong Choices

So far we've looked at problems others place on us. Sometimes, though, we feel weighed down by our own mistakes. After one concert, a shy, young woman of around 18 came and stood nearby as I talked with some other people. Finally, after everyone else left, I turned to her. I saw the deep, relentless sorrow in her eyes. "Is there something on your mind, honey?" I asked gently.

"The baby would be a year old now, if…if I hadn't had the abortion…" She said she was a Christian, and she told me she'd believed bearing a child out of wedlock would hurt her Christian testimony. She'd felt she had no other choice.

I asked her if anyone at the clinic had prepared her for the feelings of loss, regret, and mourning for the child they'd torn from her body.

"No," she replied. "If I'd known it was going to be like this…Oh, God, have mercy on me…If I'd known, I wouldn't have done it. Now I often just sit and hold my childhood baby doll and cry."

The jagged scars on her wrist and lower arm made it clear she'd attempted other ways to end her sorrow as well.

The Way Out of Pain and Sorrow

Scripture portrays marriage as two people becoming one—uniting spiritually, emotionally, and physically in one love and one purpose. It's not difficult to see how much harder this uniting becomes when one or both of the partners still writhe in pain from wounds inflicted in the past. These wounds can keep a couple from settling into the oneness God wants for them.

At one time Steve and I needed to move, but we weren't able to sell our first home before we had to leave. During the entire time our first house was on the market, we weren't able to feel settled in our new location. The unfinished business of an unsold house kept us from feeling free to rest peacefully elsewhere. Once while we talked about this, Steve mused, "Do you suppose it works the same for marriages? Do wounds from the past keep people from settling in and feeling at home in their marriage?"

The answer is "Yes, indeed!" Coming together loaded down with excess baggage is about as easy as a man and woman trying to hug with a couple of huge suitcases between them. The good news is that it is possible to find healing for these wounds. How? By forgiving the one who has wounded you.

Ouch! I know. That wasn't what you wanted to hear, was it? And believe me, I realize from experiences in my own life how very, *very* difficult forgiving someone can be, especially when you've been hurt deeply again and again. That doesn't make me back down on the truth though. I don't apologize for insisting that you must forgive the people who have hurt you. God's Word teaches there's *no other way to healing* except by the surgical removal of bitterness using the scalpel of forgiveness. Jesus insisted on it. He told His disciples to include this in their prayers: "Forgive us our debts, *as we also have forgiven our debtors*" (Matthew 6:12). Scripture doesn't say whether any of the disciples argued with Him about His strict stand on forgiveness. Jesus must have known they were arguing mentally because He went on to say, "If you forgive others for their transgressions, your heavenly Father will also forgive you. But if you do not forgive others, then your Father will not forgive your transgressions" (verses 14-15). Christ *requires* that we pardon those who have hurt us if we expect to receive His pardon for our own wrongdoings.

But here's the good news. When we choose to forgive, we're writing our own ticket to freedom. One woman whose father sexually abused her during most of her childhood, once said to me, "I won't be free of his influence until he dies." But even his death won't set her free because she's tied to this man and his evil ways by bonds of bitterness that even his death can't break. She believes it's the abuse that is still ruining her life, but I disagree. Though she's been terribly wounded, God's power and grace is more than sufficient to comfort and heal her spirit. He can even bring beauty and strength into her life despite the terrible violation she suffered. But He will do so only when she asks Him to help her and she chooses to follow His guidance. And, according to Scripture, that will include responding to her abuser with forgiveness rather than bitterness. Then, and only then, will the man's hold on her be broken forever.

One thing needs to be made clear. We don't forgive those who've hurt us because they *deserve* it. We forgive because Christ has forgiven us. We are told to pass on that grace to those who have wronged us. That's why the apostle Paul tells us, "Get rid of all bitterness, rage and anger...forgiving each other, *just as in Christ God forgave you*" (Ephesians 4:31-32 NIV).

And when we forgive, we're certainly not saying the abuser was right in what he or she did. We're not letting the person off the hook. We're not whitewashing evil behaviors by renaming them "weaknesses," or "unfortunate choices," or "mistakes." Look back over the baggage we've described already. A father who terrorizes his children...a spouse who commits adultery...a friend who betrays—these acts aren't just "problems." They need to be called what they are—sin—without denial or covering up.

But sin must be forgiven. We need to pardon the offender for Jesus' sake, for the person's sake, and also for our *own* sake. (That doesn't mean we allow the abuse to continue.) Bitterness that's allowed to take root and grow in us will have no effect on the abusers, but it will cripple us. And if allowed to continue, it can eventually snuff out our lives.

One woman who'd been violently molested said,

> Whenever I thought about forgiving this person who violated me so cruelly, I could not let that hurt go because he deserved to pay. The truth is, my thoughts of hatred and bitterness had absolutely no effect on him, but they were tearing my life apart.

This woman suffered crippling arthritis, broken relationships, and immense depression, which didn't begin to change until she decided that with God's help, she would begin actively to forgive her offender. She wrote,

If I had a thought of hatred for this man—and I had many—I'd acknowledge the thought (not deny it), and then I would thank the Lord for how it would drive me to Him.

Then I would concentrate on God's love and His ability to forgive *me* no matter what I had done. I especially worked on thinking of Scripture passages that helped me focus on God's truth—like 1 John 4:7 that says, "Dear friends, let us love one another, for love comes from God." It helped me to choose to forgive this man.

After all this, I would pray for his salvation, and then ask God to give me divine forgiveness from my heart. It seemed I had to go through the same process a hundred times a day for awhile. But after I relinquished my hatred, God did a real healing in my life.

The crippling arthritis has left my body. No longer am I victimized by the severe pain. God, in His infinite love and mercy, brought into my life the most precious man ever born, a man of godly character who loves me in purity and respect. We have been married for over 10 years and have 2 beautiful children. We have had no trouble in communicating our mutual love sexually. In fact, I believe God has blessed us in an extra abundance in that area of our marriage because of the pain of the past. He and He alone, can bring life from death, beauty from ashes. And that's what He's done in my life.

Does this lady's resolution of her life-damaging experience sound too good to be true? If so, I should tell you I am that lady, and my story is true. I'm not the only one who has found wholeness in the face of brokenness. Others have written to us that they too have found the same freedom I did by choosing the way of forgiveness. Here are just a few of their testimonies:

- I've been able to forgive my father and I've learned to go to God to supply my needs as my "heavenly Father." I no longer have to seek men to fill that role in my life, for God has filled that longing.

- Through prayer I have lost the bitterness I had toward my ex-husband. I have forgiven him. A crisis occurred [when he abandoned our family]. But we have survived and are actually better for having gone through it.

- Even though I went through a really hard time, I finally was able to allow God to heal me of feelings of rejection and the bitterness that went with it. I [now] believe God works all things for the good to them that love Him. Through my state of depression He has blessed me greatly. My husband and I are closer than ever. I still have some bad days, but I'm trusting the Lord to help me overcome my problems. I am taking one day at a time, and I know that I'm going to be all right, thanks to God.

For some, the one they needed to forgive was themselves. You might forgive others but never let yourself go free. Pardoning yourself is just as essential to finding peace as forgiving a person who has wronged you. We've also received many messages of hope from those who had to make this important step:

- I had an abortion in 1972. Even though I knew I was forgiven by God, I had not forgiven myself or my husband for what we had done. We were not married yet, and I didn't want to hurt Christian family members by me being pregnant—so we chose abortion (which is a decision we wish now we had not made!). That night after we talked I forgave myself and my husband, and he forgave me and himself. That was a new beginning for our marriage.

- After having gone through a divorce and having lived
apart from the Lord during that time, I had a lot of
guilt cluttering up my heart. I couldn't let go of it, even
though I knew I had been forgiven. But I finally let Jesus
into my "secret place." And after letting go of that guilt,
I wanted to run and jump and shout for joy! For the
first time I felt as if I were whole again and able to hold
my head up and be proud that Jesus loves me, a terrible sinner. I felt like such a failure because I had a failed
marriage in my past. While some of my past is certainly
nothing to be proud of, I could be proud of the fact that
Jesus forgave me, died for me, and loves me still.

The Cure for Excess Baggage

Are you struggling under the load of excess baggage? Let Christ
set you free from bondage to the wounds of the past. He wants you
to know a satisfying *today* and an even brighter *tomorrow*. He came
to set captives free, including you. Allow Him to liberate you so you
can be free to love. To illustrate His willingness and ability to make
all the needed difference in a wounded life, consider the following
true story in lyric form:

Innocence Lost

A young girl, nine years old
Running to that swimming hole
With her family to spend another summer day
There was one who'd meet them there
He sat in his easy chair
He'd watch the kids and say, "I'll keep them safe"

He would often bring them treats—
lemonade and homemade sweets
But on that day he brought a hidden secret
Oh, the things she learned that day
While the other children played
Would change her life forever

Just a child, innocence lost
Stolen smile; oh what a cost
She's going to need the healing hand of Christ
That catches every tear she cries
When she's alone with her thoughts…of innocence lost

Years went by, but in her world
She was still that little girl
Down by that old pond all alone
She was so afraid to tell,
So she just learned to hide it well
Behind a life that felt so wrong

But then one day she met the One
Who sees beyond what has been done
And heals the pain that comes with hidden secrets
When she told Him everything
In her heart she heard Him say,
"Child, your faith has made you whole"

Just a child; innocence lost
Stolen smile; so great a cost
But she found the loving hand of Christ
That catches every tear she cries
She's no longer alone with her thoughts…
of innocence lost[1]

Different, Not Difficult

by Steve

*I*f you want to reduce a boulder to rubble, you could stuff a dozen sticks of dynamite under it and let 'er blow. Or you could put a kid armed with a little hammer next to that boulder and let him *tap, tap, tap* on it. Give that kid enough time, and you'd find him sitting next to a pile of powder every bit as fine as the one the dynamite produced.

The same principle works in marriage. There are as many homes disintegrated by the *rat-a-tat-tat* of unresolved irritations as by the dynamite blast of an affair or alcoholism or abuse. Don't you know couples who wound up divorcing over her impulse purchase of a coffee table or his surprise decision to take a fishing vacation? I do.

But, of course, it wasn't really the furniture or the fishing lures that broke them up. Those were likely just the final irritation in a long, long string of differences that never got resolved. You see, it's not the differences themselves, but what we *do* about our differences—large *and* small—that will decide our marital destiny. If you can't settle the "Battle of the Toothpaste Tube," you surely won't be able to negotiate your way through the major war zones in marriage—sex, money, in-laws, and child-rearing, to name a few.

Every couple has differences. Speaking personally, I find many of the differences between Annie and me delightful. They constitute several of the reasons I married her. For instance, because of her talent for decorating, she's made our house into a lovely home. Me? I was never much for fussing with details like pictures on the walls or doodads on the mantel. In fact, before I married Annie my definition of a well-kept bedroom was one where I threw all my dirty clothes into just one corner. After we were married, Annie informed me that the four posts on our bed were *not* put there to be mannequins. But they were so convenient sticking up like that, so until then I'd just pick one, undress beside it, and hang my clothes on it. Yes, all four posts were usually fully clothed at any given time. In light of my housekeeping handicap, you can imagine my pleasure as a newlywed when I came home to a place where the flower boxes had things growing in them and the refrigerator *didn't*.

There was, however, a side to Annie's decorating gift I wasn't prepared for. All that pretty paper she loves to adorn the walls… it doesn't just appear there by itself. The stuff has to be measured, and cut, and matched, and pasted, and hung. There I'd be, hanging from a ladder trying to position an eight-foot strip of this wet, gooey paper on the wall—making sure it was straight and, at the same time, trying to match it up to the teeny-tiny flowers on the last piece, which were, of course, only about as big as fly specks. And just as I was getting the last strip glued down flat, I'd hear from down below, "This looks so wonderful, Steve. Let's do Heidi's room too!" (I know a woman who insists if God hadn't intended divorce, He never would have invented wallpaper. There are days I've wondered if maybe she doesn't have a point.)

I discovered also that just because Annie's furniture arrangements looked great, that didn't mean she intended them to stay that way. Like the true interior decorator she is, Annie insists that "perfect" can be made more perfect, which, of course, necessitates constant change. Today the teacups might be in the dining room hutch. Tomorrow, they may have been moved to the kitchen. I can never expect to walk into a darkened room in our house and plunk into my recliner because in the time it took me to go outside to get the newspaper, Annie may have decided the living room grouping needed the recliner more than the family room did. Heaven help me if I ever go blind and have to find my way around our house! A trip across the living room would leave me with severe shin fractures. Have you ever wondered where the expression "Here today, gone tomorrow" came from? I'm sure the writer came up with it while watching Annie in decorating mode.

I'm sure Annie could come up with her own Jekyll and Hyde stories of our differences. She does share one example often. She says one of the things she loved about me when we were dating was the aura of excitement I always exuded. Physical danger scares her more than it does me, so she loved my masculine daring. No one told her, however, that this "masculine daring" causes me to push a tank of gas just as far as it will go. It's "man against meter," so the closer I come to lurching into the gas station with nothing left in the tank but fumes, the more I feel like a winner.

In my own defense, I've never actually run out of gas. I have come pretty close though. One day we left home early for a Sunday-morning concert. We were on the highway before I realized I'd never seen the gas gauge *that* far below empty. And because we'd left so early, I knew no gas stations would be open yet. I also knew we couldn't go a half mile on what was left in that tank. We were either going to have to chance getting stalled on the highway or stop at the station I could see ahead and wait for it to open.

I pulled into the station but being too proud to admit the gauge had bested me this time, I cheerily announced to my family that we were going to "stop here and rest a bit." The "bit" turned out to be 45 minutes, which was when the manager arrived to pump gas. My family wasn't fooled in the slightest by my "resting" routine.

I also pull similar stunts when we get lost on a trip. We're not sure where we are, and suddenly it becomes "man against the wilderness." It's up to me to find a way through that maze of freeways to bring my little family safely home. Stop and ask for directions? Did Lewis and Clark stop at a Standard Station? Would Davy Crockett have called AAA? My adrenalin starts pumping, my hands tighten on the steering wheel, and we strike out to make it all on our own. (Annie points out that we never heard Mrs. Crockett's side of the story. How many church suppers did she have to walk into late because Davy wouldn't ask directions? And how many times did she find herself without horsepower because Davy insisted on seeing how far their old nag could go without food?)

Character quirks. *Everyone* has them. And the ones we found most charming in one another when we first met are usually the same ones that later can force a wedge between us. That's why it matters that we learn *how* to deal with them early so our marriages don't get irritated to death.

Irritations: Share Them with Love

To settle our irritations, Annie and I always begin by applying a truth so obvious that when I say it you're going to wonder if I'm a parolee from the State Home for the Dense. I'm going to say it anyway. Your partner has to know how he or she is irritating you *before* any change can be considered or take place. If you're irritated by something, you need to *say so*.

I told you it would sound obvious. But you'd be surprised at the people we meet that overlook something so obvious. We know lots of women who believe the Bible's challenge to submit to their husbands means they should never voice any displeasure or irritations or disagreement. If they do, they're swamped with guilt for not acting submissively enough.

Others we know won't bring up their gripes because they believe God wants them to be peacekeepers. But Jesus never told us to *keep* the peace; instead, He said we're to be *peacemakers*. *Peacekeepers* avoid conflict at any cost, but *peacemakers* take an honest look at differences and seek ways to come to mutually acceptable resolutions. To a peacekeeper, conflict is the enemy. To a peacemaker, conflict simply presents an opportunity to communicate and compromise so both sides can do a better job of understanding and giving to each other.

When I married Annie, I asked her to be sure she always told me when something in our life displeased her. She's been faithful to do that, and I've been glad. Like many men, I'm not very sharp in threading my way through the intricacies of emotional communication. For the most part, I knew I would need help to know if things weren't right. (I do remember once when I got it right. I asked Annie if something was wrong, and she said no. I had the good sense to not accept her answer that time. Of course, when she insisted everything was all right her voice was as flat as a three-day-old glass of ginger ale, and the look on her face would have made a death-row inmate look happy by comparison. I may be slow, but no one's *that* slow!)

So because Annie and I have open communication regarding irritations, she's told me how she feels about my antics with the fuel gauge and pushing the envelope. I now know how she prefers the toilet paper to come off the roller, and that it makes her crazy when I leave my beard trimmings in the sink. (She tells me it looks as if our sink is growing hair—gray hair at that. I have to agree with her. That thought is pretty disgusting.)

Thankfully, when Annie expresses an irritation, she makes it easy for me to hear because she's also faithful to practice the primary "three nevers" every couple should know and implement:

- Annie never couples her irritation with *character assassination*. For instance, she never says things like "What kind of slob would leave half his beard in the sink?"

- She never makes her complaint *a moral judgment*. For example, she doesn't hold her nose in the air and sarcastically say, "I'm sure a really *godly* husband wouldn't get us lost like this at 11:30 at night and refuse to ask for help."

- She never *insists her solution is the only way* to resolve the difference or issue. She's open to ideas and negotiation.

No, when Annie comes to me with an irritation, it's usually in a quiet, supportive spirit. "Steve, when you leave your clothes in the middle of the floor, I feel taken for granted." She keeps her complaint to just one issue, and makes it clear how deeply it bothers her; but she also practices the kind of love that "doesn't insist on its own way." She gives me a chance to work with her toward a mutually agreeable solution.

Because Annie approaches me in such a kind and gentle manner, she encourages me to want to work toward a solution. Annie practices two *essentials* that also help: She's as quick (actually, quicker) to *point out what she likes about me* and *how I please her* as she is to voice irritations.

Please don't get the idea that sniffing out conflicts is the wife's job in a marriage. It certainly isn't. But as I said earlier, Annie seems to have a relational seismograph that picks up rumbles between us that I don't feel until they've became a quake big enough to flatten half of San Francisco. I believe many women share that capacity and gift.

The three "nevers" plus the two essentials work equally well regardless of whether the husband or the wife is the irritated one. Using them while you share your beef with your partner can keep a minor dogfight from escalating into World War III. It can help you get the coffee-table conflicts out on the table so you can resolve them *before* they get so big you wind up dividing the furniture in a divorce settlement.

When Your Spouse Won't Budge

When and how to talk about what irritates you sounds good, doesn't it? You simply voice in a calm and gracious manner your concern to your partner, and together you find a solution you're both happy with. That works great…part of the time. But if you believe that's how it's always going to be, I have news you aren't going to like. Sometimes your partner simply isn't going to change.

This reminds me of the story of a man piloting his ship through dark and stormy waters. Up ahead he spotted the light of another ship headed right toward him.

He grabbed the ship's radio and bellowed into it, "Collision imminent. Veer 10 degrees north!"

The radio speaker crackled and a voice came through, "*You* veer 10 degrees south."

"I am an admiral!" the first man said. "Now you veer 10 degrees north."

"I'm just a midshipman," the voice from the darkness returned, "but *you* still must veer 10 degrees south."

Now the light ahead was dangerously close. "This is a *battleship!*" the admiral said as menacingly as he could. "Now veer 10 degrees north."

"You veer 10 degrees south," the voice said evenly, "because *this* is a lighthouse."

Sometimes the behaviors that irritate us aren't going to change—maybe not now and maybe not ever. (Annie could illustrate this point for you. You see, just last week I nearly ran out of gas…again!) So what's a spouse to do with an irritation that doesn't go away? You've probably heard the prayer attributed to Reinhold Neibuhr that goes like this:

> God, grant me the serenity
> to accept the things I cannot change,
> courage to change the things I can,
> and wisdom to know the difference.

The things we can't change about our mates, we have to accept if we're to have peace. Acceptance is not the same as resignation. You can recognize resignation when you hear the sounds of pitiful pouting and the moans of martyrdom. ("He treats me so badly [*sigh*]. But I married him, so I guess I have to put up with it.")

Acceptance comes easier when we don't expect perfection of our mates. Annie knew from the start she married an imperfect man. (Well, maybe a *nine,* but still imperfect.) And it helps to keep the big picture of all our mates' good qualities in view. The Bible tells us to "dwell on the fine, good things in others" (Philippians 4:8 TLB). That's advice to heed if we want to keep irritations in the right perspective.

Annie shared how our conflict over Christmas celebrations could have led to a major rift between us. One of the things that helped her accept me when I'd failed miserably to meet her expectations was reminding herself of the big picture. She told me later, "I knew you were acting like a jerk about Christmas. But then I thought, 'So what!' I considered everything else I know about you—your devotion to the Lord and all you do for our family. I decided it wasn't worth messing up the wonderful relationship we have the other 364 days a year just because of Christmas Day."

That same principle is what helps me accept Annie's continual fussing over home decor placement and my constantly bumped shins on the "floating" furniture. An occasional stumble over a footstool is a small price to pay for the pleasure of living in a home that's as inviting as she's made ours. Even if her continual rearranging of the nest didn't produce such lovely results, coping with the results would still be a small inconvenience compared to the privilege of sharing my life with a woman who shows so much love and grace.

Annie reminds me too that if we let them, these irritations can build character instead of walls. (Looks to me like she's going to be *quite* a character by the time she's done living with me!) But she makes a good point. Remember our definition of romance? Having a servant's heart and looking for ways to give to the other out of love for Christ. These irritations can be prime places to give—and sometimes we need to give in a way that costs us dearly. When we do, we're loving our partners with Christ's love, and He won't let our giving go unrewarded. Sometimes the return He gives comes in the form of changing our mates. Other times the return is that He changes us to be more patient, or to see the irritation in a different light, or to turn it into a positive bonding point in our marriages. Have you noticed that many of the moments we laugh about now as couples originated in irritations that used to drive us crazy? For some irritations, laughter is the best resolution.

But there's something you need to know. Annie and I *never* make a joke to others about the things that irritate us unless we *both* have reached the point where we think it's funny. Jokes about your spouse can easily become thinly veiled attacks or excuses for sarcasm and ridicule. With a quick wit, you can say what you've always wanted to say, throw up your hands in innocence, and claim, "I was only kidding. Why are you always so oversensitive?" Be warned! There's probably no quicker way to ruin romance.

As Annie and I have thought about dealing with irritations, we realize we're very fortunate. Both Annie and I grew up in homes where our parents provided good examples of how to deal with differences. My dad, for instance, never yelled at my mother. Sometimes they whispered intently—very intently—but there was no hollering. I have never heard my parents call each other names, demean each other, stomp out of the house in a rage, or strike one another. When differences came up, they were discussed without nagging, sulking, whining, or threatening. I'm very grateful for such a rich legacy.

Your background may be different, or perhaps your mate's is. Even if that's so, Jesus Christ can be your role model as you notice the way He spoke the truth in love as recorded in the Scriptures. And you may want to look for Christian couples who also model His ways. Dealing with irritations requires some good coping and communication skills. Thankfully, if you don't have them you can learn them. That's the purpose of resources such as Marriage Encounter,

FamilyLife Conferences, and multitudes of books and recordings you'll find at Christian bookstores. We've found that these teachings have helped us use our irritations as opportunities to grow closer instead of allowing them to become threats to our love.

When all these techniques don't work to resolve the scuffles over irritations, another tool is to remind yourself of the brevity of life. Who knows how long the Lord will give you to be with each other? In light of how quickly our lives speed by, irritations are, after all, very little.

6

God, Marriage, and Money

by Annie

*B*efore he would perform our wedding, our minister sat Steve and me down to soak up his standard, 12-minute, premarital pep talk. (Little did we know that 12 *weeks* wouldn't have been enough to prepare us for the leap into matrimony we were about to make. Fortunately, we looked at life from a happy mix of youth and ignorance. We listened expectantly to the 12 minutes of advice that would guarantee us 50 or 60 years of romantic bliss.)

Most of what that minister said we heartily said "Amen!" to... but not everything. "One of the biggest sources of potential problems in your marriage," he told us, "will be *money.*" We were too polite to disagree, but when he said that, we knew he couldn't be talking about us because *we didn't have any.* How do you have problems with something you don't have? And since our career plans centered around a Christian music ministry that offered no set income or guarantee, we didn't figure we'd ever have enough money to cause struggles.

We were right about not having money. During our first year of marriage our gross income came to $3000. (That *is* gross, isn't it. The median income in the United States way back then was

$11,800.) Unfortunately, we found to our dismay that no marriage is immune to struggles over the green stuff. We had things to learn *together* about having and not having money. God started with us individually, teaching each of us that *He* was our provider. The financial lessons for me began with my desire for a washer and dryer.

As newlyweds, we parked ourselves in a garage that had been converted into a tiny, two-room apartment. Paying the rent and keeping our old '50 Chevy running ate up most of our meager funds. That's why it seemed absolutely out of the question to talk to Steve about buying a washer and dryer. I hated lugging our clothes to the Laundromat, but I knew that, with our income, buying laundry equipment was as possible as buying a Mercedes. Telling Steve about my desire would only burden him because there was no way he could come up with the extra money.

What was a new bride to do? I could wheedle, wail, whine, or find work to earn money for a washer and dryer. But the thought came to mind that I had a better place to start than any of these. I could pray! God promised He'd provide all our needs, so I decided to start by asking Him. In the same way a little child would come to her father, I went to God and told Him about my desire for a washer and dryer.

Zap! Friends offered us their used set. I was ecstatic when they moved that equipment into our carport. What could be easier than this? Shoot up a little request and down float two Maytags—used but still usable! Before I'd even had a chance to tell Steve about my prayer and its instantaneous answer, my generous husband remembered a couple we knew who'd just had a baby. Surely they needed the washer and dryer more than we did. So he up and gave the appliances to them. I cried to myself while I watched them load *my* washer and dryer onto the truck.

Now what? Maybe I'd missed something in the way I prayed, so I tried it again. And sure enough, not even a month later a friend stopped us after church to ask if we needed a new washer and dryer.

New! I thought. *No wonder God allowed the first set to be given away. He had something better for me.* I was just drawing a deep breath to shout "Hallelujah!" when Steve informed our friend that of course we needed the washer and dryer, but he knew a couple with a new baby who were making do with an old set. Surely they needed the new appliances more than we did.

I couldn't believe my ears! Were all the new parents in the world going to have to own laundry equipment before I could be set free from lugging loads to the Laundromat? When our finances seemed just a bit better, I told Steve how much I wanted laundry appliances, and he agreed it was a valid need. So we went to the store and applied for credit. We ordered a brand-new, beautiful Maytag duo. The night before they were to be delivered, I was so excited I barely slept.

But they never came. Before the delivery truck showed up, the store called to tell us our credit application had been rejected. I was so low I had to look up to see the bottom. The three answers to my prayer had been "almost yeses" that slid away into "no's." Had I been foolish to pray? Was I praying wrongly? Could I expect God to get involved in our finances or not? Not knowing what else to do, I continued to pray for a washer and dryer—and patience and understanding.

I'm pleased to report that God *did* provide a washer and dryer— and some very interesting side benefits too. A few months later, I became pregnant, and with the pregnancy came fainting spells. One day at the Laundromat, the heat got to me and I passed out, hitting my head on the concrete floor when I fell. I woke up in the hospital. I had a concussion. The doctor told Steve, "This woman is never to do laundry in a hot, old Laundromat again." So the lady who hated Laundromats was medically banished from them forever, leaving Steve to do laundry detail. (And they say there's no justice in the world!)

A few weeks later, Steve learned from a neighbor about a resource that would allow us to buy the exact equipment we'd almost received before at *half* price. One night he took me out to dinner. He'd secretly arranged for his friends to put the new washer and dryer in place while we were gone. When we came home, there they waited, greeting me in all their shiny porcelain glory. There was even a single red rose sitting in a vase on the washer. (Who says laundry can't be romantic?)

A year after I began to pray, God provided beautiful, new laundry appliances. The *way* He chose to work put me through the wringer (pun intended), but I came away with lessons I've used again and again in the years since. What did I learn?

God wants to provide for us, and He is more than able to do so. Both Steve and I needed to ask Him to help us. God doesn't always provide in the exact way I envision, and He doesn't always act on my timetable. But if He seems slow to work or says no, I count on the likelihood that He's got a larger and greater good in mind for me.

In our case, because God didn't say yes to me at once, another family was able to enjoy first a used washer and dryer and then new ones. Steve and I got the joy of giving generously—twice!—at a time when we didn't have much cash to give. And best of all, we were spared dependence on using credit as a way to provide for our needs. It can easily become a way of life to look to MasterCard instead of the true Master for our provision. Why wait on the Lord when a 2"x3" plastic rectangle can free us from the Laundromat right now? Because we couldn't get credit, we had no choice but to wait. And when we waited, God had a chance to work and remind us He could and would provide. And He tacked on no interest or carrying charges!

This experience with the washer and dryer helped my faith grow. And I needed it during the week when, after we paid all our bills, we had only five dollars left over to buy groceries. Now, I can squeeze a nickel till Thomas Jefferson winces, but I knew there was no way I could feed the two of us for a week on five dollars. So I prayed, reminding the Lord He'd promised His people would not be left to beg for bread. It came to my mind to ask Him for six invitations to dinner that week, so I did. That settled, I went to the store and spent the five dollars on a loaf of bread, a carton of milk, a box of cereal, and a pound of bologna (five bucks went a long way in those days). It was all we needed to cover breakfast and lunch for the week.

And then, although it had never happened before (or since, for that matter), the phone began to ring. To my amazement, we received six calls, each caller inviting us to dinner for a different night that week.

Another time when we were in need, Steve and I walked out on our porch and found a box of groceries there. Still another time, money came anonymously in the mail. And there were unexpected opportunities to work for pay.

Those early lessons taught me the most important principle I needed to learn about money: *God* is our provider, and a faithful provider He is. While I was learning the "Lessons of the Laundry and the Lunches," God had a financial training program going for Steve as well.

When we first married, our apartment also lacked a refrigerator, so we bought one. And what a refrigerator! For 15 dollars we came home with a round-faced, 1965 model Frigidaire. Though it kept things sufficiently cool, it had two annoying habits: It "walked" around the kitchen due to how it vibrated when it was running and it didn't defrost itself. (Steve discovered this second unfortunate fact the morning he opened the freezer and found it so thoroughly frosted up, he couldn't fit a Popsicle inside.) In a good wifely fashion, I said I'd defrost it.

"Great, sweetheart, great!" Steve said. "Just one thing. Don't jab that frozen stuff out with a knife. You may be tempted to rush the process along; but whatever you do, *don't* go poking into that freezer box with anything sharp."

Well, two hours later I was on the phone to my husband. "Steve…

honey, I was defrosting and (cough, cough) using a knife. And I, uh, I punctured something, sweetheart. The refrigerator just made a long *swh-h-h-h-h-h* sound." Of course, what I'd done was punctured the freon tube that circles the ice box when I jabbed into it with my knife, and that noise was the life draining from our refrigerator.

Steve didn't say anything but I'm sure I heard muffled choking noises on the other end of the line. When he spoke, he was the model of rage restrained.

"Now, sweetheart," he said evenly, "you know we can't afford another refrigerator, so you'll have to do the best you can." And he told me to take the money we had and get ice and a Styrofoam cooler from the Hot Stop grocery down the street. Then he hung up—most likely before he said something he knew he'd regret later.

But even as he was putting down the receiver, a man stuck his head in Steve's door at the church where he was working, and said, "My wife and I just got the call we've been waiting for about our clearance to leave for Guatemala to work there for a year. We need to get rid of some things quickly. Do you need a refrigerator?"

Faster than NASCAR driver Jimmy Johnson, Steve zoomed across town in a truck he borrowed from our church and picked up the refrigerator. It was enormous. It didn't walk around, it had an icemaker, and, best of all, it was self-defrosting. *And* it was full of food. Not only did Steve not have to wait for God to provide, but that time he didn't even have to pray.

Seeing such dramatic provisions didn't keep my normally levelheaded husband from having his own moments of financial panic. One time he got a call from our accountant…on April 12. And it was the call you never want to get three days before taxes are due.

"I hate to break the news to you, Steve," the man began, "but you owe some extra money this year."

"How much?" Steve asked.

And after Steve got up off the floor, he told the man, "We don't have that kind of money."

"Do the best you can," the accountant said. "You've got three days."

The main reason we were caught so terribly off guard and failed to have the money set aside for our taxes was because we were under the impression that those earning under a certain amount were exempt from paying them. What we failed to account for was that regardless of how little we earned, we were still required to pay the Social Security tax.

I'd like to report that Steve responded to the unexpected call with a jubilant cry of faith, but that wasn't so. He crawled off to the bedroom and slumped on the edge of the bed. He told me later he sat there wondering what it was going to be like in jail. Thankfully, God came to our rescue. That afternoon the band Steve played in got an invitation to sing in place of another person who'd taken ill. Steve got back from the concert the night of April 14 and wrote out a check for the taxes.

Are you starting to think we believe it's important to trust God for your finances? If so, you're right! We believe it so strongly for two reasons. First, we're not very sophisticated in financial matters and know we need all the help we can get. Second, and more important, we believe it because the Bible says that's how God intends things to work. He never planned for us to worry and stew over money. Jesus said our Father wants to care for us as completely, just as He does for the ravens and the lilies (Luke 12:24,27). He wants us to be free to love Him completely and to enjoy the life He created us for.

Two of the ways we circumvent letting Him handle our finances is by refusing to wait for Him to act and not waiting for provision to be made His way.

The Need for "Wait" Training

"Wait" is a four-letter word. And today that's especially true when it comes to material things. It's not uncommon for newly married couples to look at all the stuff their parents have crammed into their attic, their garage, and the rented storage building down the road and believe that is success. The newlyweds think they're failures if they haven't acquired within two years of marriage what it took their folks 20 or 30 years to accumulate.

The push to have it all *now* creates at least two pitfalls that are easy for any couple to fall into. The first is what Steve calls the "Shop-like-a-Bull Syndrome." In other words, feeling rosy about the future you *charge* everything. When we didn't have money for a washer and dryer, what did we think of? Buy now and pay later, of course. But charging is a lot like chocolate. Just a taste makes you crazy for more…and more…*and more.*

We heard about a husband who jokingly said that his American Express card was stolen, but he refused to try to find it because the thief was using it less than his wife did. Because of the entrapment inherent in credit caused by the compounding interest charges, Steve and I decided to pay cash as we go. We only use our credit cards when we know we can pay the balance in full at the end of the month. And if an emergency comes up and we charge something but can't follow-through on our end-of-the-month payment commitment, we agreed together not to charge again until the balance reads zero. By doing this, we're not only protecting ourselves from living beyond our means, but we've saved a bundle in interest! Another benefit of limiting our use of credit is that it forces us to wait on God for His provision and His timing.

Another financial pitfall for couples is the "Double-Your-Income, Double-Your-Fun" snare. When both husband and wife earn paychecks, it's tempting to base the family's lifestyle on the assumption that both incomes will always be available. But life can change quickly. One spouse loses a job, an illness hits, the wife gets pregnant. The result? Increased expenses yet half the income to meet them.

Steve and I don't have two independent incomes, but if you do, we encourage you to consider budgeting your necessities (mortgage payment, groceries, and the like) using just one of your salaries. The second paycheck can then be used to save for a house, make investments, or go towards items not as essential as food and shelter. We've always had a savings account. Even that first year together when we made very little, we managed to save $200. No matter how small the savings may seem, make yourselves set aside some money. It will add up.

We also give a portion of our income to God's work. Whether the checks we receive are $100 or $10,000, we always pay God's share first because we want to and because we believe keeping God's share would make us vulnerable to attacks by the devil. God wants us to serve Him rather than seeking after material wealth. In fact, there are thousands of references on how to handle money in the Bible, and many of Jesus' parables dealt with the subject of finances. Mishandling finances and failing to plan for the future can have a devastating effect on the marriage. Consider these statistics:

- "37 percent of marital problems are born from financial situations."[1] God's Word *encourages* us to "let no debt remain outstanding, except the continuing debt to love one another, for whoever loves others has fulfilled the law" (Romans 13:8 NIV).

- "70 percent of all consumers live paycheck to paycheck."[2] Facing the possibility of running out of money before the end of the month adds stress and unrest to family life. God's Word *admonishes* us to plan ahead. "Suppose one of you wants to build a tower. Won't you first sit down and estimate the cost to see if you have enough money to complete it?" (Luke 14:28 NIV).

- "The average family would have to use a credit card to pay a $1,500 unexpected expense."[3] The effect of accumulating debt leads couples further and further into financial trouble. God's Word *warns*, "The rich rule over the poor, and the borrower is slave to the lender" (Proverbs 22:7 NIV).

- "Nearly half of all Americans (46 percent) have less than
  $10,000 saved for their retirement."[4] God's Word *cau-
  tions*, "The wise store up choice food and olive oil, but
  fools gulp theirs down" (Proverbs 21:20 NIV).

So often couples ask the wrong questions when it comes to considering purchases:

- "Do we have the money for this expenditure?" If people
  buy something simply because they can afford it, then
  money is their boss.

- "Do we not have the money for this expenditure?" If
  people don't make a purchase because they don't have
  the cash (or credit) available, then the lack of money is
  their master.

So what is the best question we should ask when it comes to
spending?

- "Does God want us to have this?" If God does, He will
  provide the necessary resources. Yes, there are times
  when we may have to wait on His timing for the funds,
  but when we do, we're depending on God instead of
  money.

Remember, Jesus said, "No one can serve two masters. Either
you will hate the one and love the other, or you will be devoted
to the one and despise the other. You cannot serve both God and
money" (Matthew 6:24 NIV).

Making It Through the Money Maze

So far I've told you a lot about what Steve and I learned individually about money, and I've let you in on some things we agree about.
But it's not always financial bliss under the Chapman roof. The premarital warning about money being a sure source of tension for a

couple wasn't wrong. And money—how we get it and what we do with it—has caused tension for us from time to time.

I grew up in a little community where everyone knew everyone else's business. So my dad, to save himself some embarrassment, arranged with our banker to cover any outstanding checks his kids wrote. Therefore, keeping a balanced checkbook was never a burning need for me because I always knew Daddy would make up any deficits. This worked well—that is, until I married. Steve made it clear he was my husband, not my father, and that henceforth I'd need to take responsibility for recording the amounts of money I parted with.

On the whole, I've done quite well at keeping my accounts in order. But not long ago, I let things slide and we got a call from the bank. When my husband came home from paying out $45 in overdraft charges, he was not in a jovial mood, to say the least. In the tirade that followed, I found out once again how amazingly articulate Steve can be, and how completely he's able to vent his feelings.

The problem was he was dead right. And when he finished laying out his case, he leaned over, peered at me, and asked, "Will this *ever* happen again?"

I looked back at him with the same seriousness. "Yes, it will," I told him. "But not for a long, long time."

Who can stay mad at such an honest woman? Our money differences don't always end so easily, but we need to remember that finances is one area of life where couples desperately need to learn to talk together, laugh together, and keep on growing together. We live in a culture that worships things, a society where people find it easier to share their bodies than their bank accounts. In his book *The Total Money Makeover*, Dave Ramsey makes an astute observation: "People were running around, buying things they couldn't afford with money they didn't have, to impress people they didn't even like."[5] That's so true! Surely this isn't what God intended.

Money is a resource, a tool for people to use in God's service. It was intended to be our slave, not to enslave us. The stewardship of it should draw us together, not push us apart. If money squabbles are creating a rift in your marriage, it's wise to seek help. Maybe the two of you did well together during the early years when you had fewer things, but now with increased income has come more conflict. Today, Steve and I more often find ourselves on the giving end than the receiving end. Even in that we've discovered it involves responsibilities and decisions we didn't anticipate and didn't face in the early years of our marriage.

We've been greatly helped by attending money-management seminars based on the Bible. Afterward, we talked about which of the principles would work for us. (You might enjoy reading the books suggested at the end of this chapter. Use the information as a springboard for discussing your money differences and goals.) Money *can* be a major source of conflict in a marriage. But it can also be an arena for learning lessons of faith that will make you closer than ever. Finances can even provide the space God can use to do a miracle.

In recent years many of our family members and friends have been hit financially. Some have lost decade-long careers they'd depended for their livelihood as well as their retirement plans. Others lost most or all of their savings when the stock market took a dive. However, time and time again we've seen the Lord of the Harvest come through and meet their needs. The following lyric captures one of the most heartwarming and encouraging stories we've heard about God helping a family through tough economic times.

Daddy Needs a Job

Got home after dark, another long day
Trying to find some work and make some pay
Got bills that are overdue; got a family to feed
Lord knows I'll do anything,
don't want this ride for free

I went upstairs to tell my little boy good night
We said "I love you's" and before I turned out the light
He took my hand and bowed his little head
Closed his eyes and then he said

"Dear God, my daddy needs a job
Sure would make him happy and help him out a lot
He's real good at doing things and
He's got that big tool box
Dear God, my daddy needs a job"

I couldn't say a word as he finished his prayer
He said, "God, just one more thing…
Would you tell someone out there
That if my dad can fix my bike and
Build a house up in a tree
There's nothing he can't do
Tell them he's the man they need"

Then I went downstairs to tell my wife
What I heard that boy do
She smiled, handed me the phone,
And said, "Baby, it's for you"

"Dear God, my daddy needs a job
Sure would make him happy and help him out a lot
He's real good at doing things
And he's got that big tool box.
Dear God, my daddy needs a job" [6]

Recommended Financial Planning Guides

Burkett, Larry. *The Complete Financial Guide for Young Couples*. Chicago: Moody Publishers, 2002.

_____. *How to Manage Your Money*. Colorado Springs: David C. Cook, 2002.

Crosson, Russ. *8 Important Money Decisions for Every Couple*. Eugene, OR: Harvest House Publishers, 2013.

_____. *The Truth About Money Lies*. Eugene, OR: Harvest House Publishers, 2012.

Kay, Ellie. *A Woman's Guide to Family Finances*. Bloomington, MN: Bethany House Publishers, 2004.

Pegues, Deborah Smith. *30 Days to Taming your Finances*. Eugene, OR: Harvest House Publishers, 2006.

Ramsey, Dave. *Financial Peace Revisited*. New York: Viking, 2003.

White, Jeremey, Ron Blue, Charles Swindoll. *The New Master Your Money: A Step-by-Step Plan for Gaining and Enjoying Financial Freedom*. Chicago: Moody Publishers, 2004.

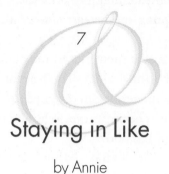

Staying in Like

by Annie

*P*eople get married because they love each other. I believe people *stay* married because they *like* each other. And because of this, I'm a great crusader for "falling in like, and staying in like" with your spouse. My penchant to promote *like* in marriage may never result in songs that make the Top 20 because "like" rhymes too easily with phrases such as "take a hike!" (Hardly the sentiments passionate ballads are made of.) On the other hand, the word "love" can be paired up with sticky sentiments like "my turtle dove" and "the stars above."

Though *love* may sound more romantic, *like* has a wonderful thing going for it. Partners who like each other have a relationship founded on respect—respect for the other person and for him- or herself as well. When respect and the "liking" it fosters flourishes in a marriage, you can bet the relationship rests on very solid ground.

How can you put more *like* in your marriage? We've found five things that work for us.

1. *Don't try to be everything to each other.* Steve is my closest friend, but he isn't my only friend. For instance, I have a good friend I can complain to on those days I feel like a failure as a parent. She

understands what I'm feeling in a way Steve doesn't simply because he isn't a mom. (One parenting authority said that though both parents love their offspring, mothers are "anchored differently" in their children. I agree.)

My friend is gracious enough to let me unload my frustrations, and when she needs to do the same, I'm there for her. Her friendship meets relational needs Steve wasn't designed to fill. An added bonus is that I have an outlet besides Steve, so he doesn't have to carry the weight of all my ups and downs.

Steve has friends like this too. His hunting buddies provide a different kind of companionship than he gets from me. God intended that our relationship take priority over others, but He never intended that we exclaim, "Us two will do!" We're active participants in life, which includes family, friends, and a full community of brothers and sisters in the faith. They need us, and we need them.

Steve and I believe these relationships with others *enhance* our liking for each other. They add a dimension to us personally that we wouldn't get if our circle was limited to two. As we grow and experience life *individually*, our life as a couple also expands because we have more to bring to our marriage.

2. *Give each other time alone.* Yes, these words are coming from a woman who for years traded in her picket fence for a small travel van so she could be next to the man she loved. You surely have no doubts by now of the importance Steve and I put on spending time together. But it's also vital to give each other the time and space to be alone.

Steve requires occasional bouts of solitariness to recharge his emotional batteries. It's easy to spot when he's been around people (even me) too much because his creativity dries up. He needs time to tromp through the woods or head out to a deserted golf course. When he's ready to write music, he holes up in a motel for a few days.

I just need time when no one will ask me to make a decision. I don't have to be absolutely alone to recharge. That's why I can take off for an afternoon in a shopping mall and come back refreshed. (I was going to say I came back "all charged up," but those words make my hubby a little nervous.)

Some of our alone time is devoted to reading God's Word and praying. Though Steve and I are deeply bonded in Christ, God still sees and relates to each of us individually. He holds us accountable individually for how we obey and love Him. I am Steve's wife, yet more importantly I am God's daughter. He speaks to me. He hears my prayers. He works with me and in me—sometimes in the same way He works with Steve, but sometimes in a very different way.

Giving ourselves to God requires that each of us spend time alone with Him—reading His Word, sharing ourselves with Him in prayer, and listening for His response. Giving each other time to develop this personal intimacy with God is what helps set our love free. Our marriage matters terribly to us, but it can't be the center of our lives. Only Jesus Christ is worthy of that honor. If we don't develop our individual relationships with Him, we may be in danger of worshipping His gift of marriage instead of worshipping the Giver, Jesus Christ. This was the sin Paul warned about in the first chapter of the book of Romans, and those committing it were headed for destruction.

Jesus Christ is the glue that holds our partnership together. Colossians 1:17 says, "In Him all things hold together." Without the bonding He provides, we wouldn't have a marriage worth preserving.

3. *If you want a marriage of long-term like, be likable.* When you choose a friend, don't you look for someone who is pleasant and enjoyable to be with? I don't tend to stay in long-term friendships with people who are always negative, boring, or unhappy. I don't expect Steve to do so either. Because he's committed to Christ, committed to me through marriage before God, and he loves me, I believe Steve will never abandon me. But I want the "staying" to be as much fun for him as possible. I don't want to just be his wife; I want to be someone he'd choose as a good friend even if we weren't married. I want to be someone he likes and wants to spend time with.

The following three actions have helped us be more likeable to each other. Perhaps they will help you as well with becoming—and staying—someone your spouse will like:

- *Talk* to your spouse about his or her strengths. Others can tell me I've sung well, but when Steve says it, well, it means so much more.

- *Thank* your spouse for the big things and the little things he or she does for you. We can so easily take for granted the ways our mates serve us. Have you thanked your husband recently for how hard he works? Have you told your wife how much you appreciate the kindnesses she shows to your parents?

- *Surprise* your mate with acts of service he or she doesn't expect. This may be making your special peach cobbler for him on a night when no guests are coming. Or it could be choosing to rent a video you know she'd love even though you'd rather watch Monday Night Football.

4. *Cultivate self-respect.* Feeling good about yourself helps you be more likeable as a person. I've found that my self-respect grows most quickly when I'm stretching and growing by venturing into new challenges. For example, I surprised Steve when I bravely tackled the assembly of a very large entertainment center/bookshelf without enlisting his help. The multiple boxes it came in contained nearly a hundred pieces and an instruction manual that was a half-inch thick. Keep in mind that I'm a person who prefers a spatula over a screwdriver and considers a nail something I file and polish. But I was determined to complete the assembly.

When I finished putting the monstrous piece of furniture together (after about 6 hours and 12 blisters on my hands) Steve was quite impressed. His affirming smile told me that he liked the self-confident, daring side of me. I definitely felt more capable of taking on other challenges I'd previously dismissed as too difficult (like taking guitar lessons).

I want to share one more thing on my furniture assembly experience. I very much appreciated how Steve exercised self-control and didn't step in or try to take over. He offered to help several times but seemed to understand I was on a personal quest to do the job on my own. It's my intention to return the favor when he wants to be adventurous, even though his adventures sometimes involve more risk than I'm comfortable with. My goal is to not smother my husband's penchant for adventure, especially the kind that can contribute to his self-confidence. I want to be like the wife in this lyric we wrote.

I'm Not Your Mother

I've had a dream for a long time
There's a mountain in Montana I wanna climb
Just me and my buddy with arrows and bows
Chase that mighty elk, and go as far as we can go

Brought it up to my wife, and I couldn't believe
What that woman had to say to me
And if I tell you boys, it might bring you to tears
'Cause there ain't no sweeter words
That a man could ever hear

She said, "I'm your lover;
I'm not your mother
You wanna be a little wild
Baby, that's all right with me
Do what you wanna do
Don't wanna control you
'Cause I'm your lover;
I'm not your mother"

The day I loaded up my truck
I was just about to leave
She came and put her lovin' arms around me
I said, "You okay with this?
I just wanna make sure!"
She smiled and said,
"Honey, let me say it just once more

I'm your lover;
I'm not your mother
You wanna be a little wild
Baby, that's all right with me
Do what you wanna do
Don't wanna control you
'Cause I'm your lover;
I'm not your mother"

Then she said, "Darlin', while you're gone
I think you ought to know
Me and my girlfriends,
Got places we can go
But I'm sure you won't mind
You'll be huntin'; you'll be happy
And, honey, after all you're not my daddy!" [1]

5. *Let your respect for one another grow as you continue to openly share your hearts.* How easy it is to get so busy in the logistics of keeping life going that we fail to share our deepest thoughts and emotions with each other. That's why so often after coming home from a singing trip with our family I tell Steve, "We really need to get some couple time together!" This may sound like a paradox, I know, since we've just spent 72 hours inches away from each other in a van,

or airplane seats, or staying in quarters almost as close. But it isn't. What we have on those trips is *physical* time together. In the responsibilities of work and family, we don't have a lot of opportunities for the kind of soul exchange that keeps our hearts beating as one.

For that kind of sharing, we usually need to get away. That often means a "date"—out to dinner or maybe even staying in a motel for the night. And for these special times, we have some ground rules. We don't go to movies because we're not together to hear someone else talk. We want and we need to hear *each other*. And we don't talk about the kids or about work. We try to focus solely on each other and what's going on personally.

Sometimes asking questions helps us open up to each other. One marriage counselor has couples write their responses to the following questions for starting points: 1) What are three things I like best about our marriage? 2) What one thing would I most like to see changed in our marriage? You can see that the answers to these questions can give the couple an interesting evening together.

Steve and I also enjoy communication quizzes. Here are a dozen questions you can draw from if you need help sharing your hearts. We've found that candidly answering questions like these helps us look at parts of our life together in a new light.

1. What first attracted you to your spouse?

2. What characteristic do you most admire about your mate?

3. Name two things your spouse has done for you that you consider romantic.

4. Name one thing your spouse likes you to do for him/her.

5. What changes would you like to make in the way you relate to your spouse?

6. What changes would you like to see your spouse make in your relationship as a couple?

7. How have your parents' relationship influenced how you get along with your spouse?

8. List your spouse's greatest needs as you see them.

9. List your greatest needs.

10. If you had the power to change one thing about yourself, what would it be?

11. If you had the power to change one thing about your spouse, what would it be?

12. What do you both most need to change to keep your relationship a top priority in your lives?

Perhaps the most valuable benefit of being likable is how much it contributes to a strong, intimate friendship between you and your mate. A friendship that will endure until "death do you part." Steve took a true story and created a lyric that represents the kind of lasting friendship we both want to enjoy.

Let Me Take Her Home

We thought it would be best to put our grandma in that home
But Grandpa's heart was broken; left him all alone
We didn't think him able in the winter of his years
To give her the help she needed, but he said through his tears

"Let me take her home with me
'Cause I made a promise I have to keep
And I know that's where she'd rather be
Let me take her home
I can't leave her here alone
Let me take her home with me"

Every day he made the journey
to see the one who wore his name
He'd sit with her for hours; she never knew he came
He was her faithful friend till the close of every day
Then he would beg for mercy as they would send him away
And he'd say…

"Let me take her home with me
'Cause I made a promise I have to keep
And I know that's where she'd rather be
Let me take her home
I can't leave her here alone
Let me take her home with me"

Then one night it happened; Grandpa went home early
At least that's what the nurses assumed
But he was hiding in a closet, and when the lights went out
Quietly he slipped into her room
Then with all his strength remaining
he gathered her in his arms
His one and only love of sixty years
And down the darkened hallway to the safety of his Buick
He carried her and whispered in her ear

"I'm going to take you home with me
'Cause I made a promise I have to keep
And I know that's where you'd rather be
I'm gonna take you home
Can't leave you here alone
I'm gonna take you home with me"

Well, he proved that love was able
'cause he was with her till the end
And before the year was over
we said goodbye to him
Now they both are resting on a hill outside of town
But in the hearts of all who knew him
these words are written down
"Let me take her home with me!" [2]

Protected Love

by Steve

I've never been one to put much stock in dreams. Give me a pepperoni pizza about 10:30 at night, and I can dream the weirdest stuff, like hairpins chasing me around the room or even worse. Because that's true, I assume most of my dreams contain more messages from my digestive system than messages from the Lord. But occasionally my dreams stop me short, and their messages are so clear, so appropriate, that I know they're from God and not a gastronomical vision.

Such was the case when Annie and I were dating. During those days, I drove a big old '50 Chevy we named Sarah (Sarah, because like Abraham's wife, she was still productive in her old age). So, in my dream...

> I was driving down the interstate in Sarah, with Annie
> sitting close beside me. The day was cold—icy cold—
> so Annie reached through the steering wheel to turn up
> the heat. But the steering wheel was loaded with chrome,
> and the big buttons on Annie's coat sleeve got twisted in
> the steering wheel. As she tugged to get free, she jerked

the wheel, and the car veered to the left and down an embankment.

We careened off the road and headed toward a huge, open field. But the field was surrounded by a large chain-link fence topped with barbed wire. To the fence was attached a large, official-looking sign that warned "NO TRESPASSING!" We plowed right through the fence and came to a stop. Suddenly, everything was silent, and I thought, "What happened?"

I looked up. Ahead of us I saw a beautiful home, shining on the hill, with a concrete drive leading up to it. Then a voice said to me, "That is where I was taking you, but because you trespassed, you will not make it there." Suddenly I heard sirens wailing and government officials arrived to drag Annie and me off in opposite directions so we could never be together again.

Then I woke up! *Whew!* It didn't take two sessions with a shrink to figure out the clear warning of this dream. Annie and I were growing to love each other, and as a result our feelings were "heating up." The Lord intended that we make a beautiful life together, thus the *Better Homes and Gardens* house I saw on the hill. But there was only one way to that home—the road of purity. If we gave in to sexual involvement before our marriage, we'd be trespassers crashing through the boundary of marriage God set around sexual union. We'd miss knowing the real oneness He intended for us to enjoy.

Yes, it was a warning we needed because, like most young couples, we were beginning to encounter moments when our hormones shouted so loudly it was nearly impossible to remember all those Bible verses about fighting temptation we'd learned so diligently. Sexual desire can have such a massive pull that without God's help, we can let it take us places we never intended to go.

Do you know the biblical account of Amnon and Tamar? It's a true story of passion out of control and illustrates well the terrible price we may pay for moments of sexual pleasure outside of marriage.

Amnon was "in luv." He was sure of it. He was smitten by his desire for his beautiful sister. "He was so frustrated because of his sister Tamar that he made himself ill, for she was a virgin, and it seemed hard to Amnon to do anything to her" (2 Samuel 13:2). Now that's deep feeling! Sexual desire can be just that overwhelming. It can make rational human beings act like total morons. And if we underestimate its power, we're as foolish as the man who throws a lighted match into a barrel of gasoline and expects nothing to happen.

On the other hand, sexual desire can generate positive energy also. Scripture says that when a man and woman join themselves physically, a mysterious spiritual, emotional, and psychological bonding happens. God intended that the ones we give ourselves to would completely merge with us on more levels than just the physical. The uniqueness and beauty of a shared sexual experience was designed to be a powerful part of the glue that melds husband and wife together for the rest of their lives. And, of course, the power to create new life rests in the miracle of sexual union.

So sex is like nuclear power. It can explode, or it can be channeled. When the energy is directed toward God's purposes and within His guidelines, it generates the heat we need to love as we should, to serve as He intended, and to create as He planned. Tim Gardner, in his book *Sacred Sex*, notes:

> If you ask the average person in the pew to identify the primary purpose of sex he or she will most likely say either procreation or recreation. Of course, both are rich blessings of sex. But the essence of sexual intimacy can never be enjoyed, nor can true and lasting sexual fulfillment occur, until a wife and a husband grasp the truth that the number-one purpose of sex is neither procreation not recreation, but *unification*. And I don't mean just the unification that is inherent in physical oneness, but also the relational unity that is celebrated, created, and re-created throughout a couple's married life. This unification is the celebration of the soul-deep bond that

is present when a couple knows and experiences the certainty that are together, permanently, for a divine purpose. They know their expression of love is meant to represent the loving relationship of Jesus and His church. They know that their life together has meaning that is far greater than simply sharing a house or bearing children. [1]

But used wrongfully, sexual activity can create havoc and hurt. That's what happened with Amnon. We have the lovesick Amnon and the desirable Tamar. Onto the scene steps Amnon's friend Jonadab, with an idea to get around God's restrictions. Jonadab told him he needed a chance to be alone with Tamar. "Lie down on your bed and pretend to be ill; when you father comes to see you, say to him, 'Please let my sister Tamar come and give me some food to eat'" (2 Samuel 13:5).

So Amnon deceived his father, King David, as his friend suggested and manipulated the meeting with Tamar. After Tamar baked her special recipe and brought the bread to Amnon, he refused to eat. He ordered everyone from the room, and asked Tamar into his bedroom so he could eat from her hand. (How's that for a weak line?)

When Tamar followed him into his bedroom, he made it clear it was the baker he wanted, not the bread. "Come lie with me, my sister," he demanded.

Tamar resisted. She reminded him of the wickedness of immorality. Then she appealed to his feelings for her. "What about me?" she pleaded. "Where could I get rid of my disgrace?" And she appealed to his pride. "And what about you? You would be like one of the fools in Israel."

But none of these arguments overcame Amnon's passion so he raped her.

One thing Amnon's actions make clear: one sin leads to another sin, and another sin, and another sin. A big sin is usually preceded by a lot of little sins. I doubt that back when Amnon was first attracted to Tamar the idea of raping her entered his mind. But he said yes to the sin of getting what he wanted by deceit, he said yes to lying to his father, he said yes to lying to Tamar, he said yes to committing assault and rape. He didn't simply leap off a cliff from purity to rape; he descended there one compromise at a time.

But, to me, the most interesting part of this story is what follows. Remember that we're dealing with a man who loved this woman so desperately and completely that he became physically sick with desire for her. Now his fantasy is fulfilled. He's joined with her sexually. What response would you expect from him? Wouldn't you think his love for her would burst into full bloom?

Listen to what really happened: "Then [after the rape] Amnon hated her with intense hatred. In fact, he hated her more than he had loved her. Amnon said to her, 'Get up and get out'" (2 Samuel 13:15). And when she refused to leave, he called his servant and had her thrown out! Sexual consummation out of God's plan won't eliminate tension in a relationship. It creates more. Sin never unites; it always divides.

Counselor Roger Hillerstrom said, "Every couple coming to me for counseling who have had premarital sexual relations have had post-marital sexual adjustment problems." And he told of a young Christian woman who sat in his office telling a story he hears all too frequently.

> I don't know what happened to our relationship. When Tom and I were dating, we felt so good about each other. We had everything going for us, and we seemed to communicate so well. We did go a bit further physically than we had planned, but it all seemed so right. Now we haven't even reached our first anniversary, and we feel like strangers. We don't understand each other emotionally—and sexually, there's nothing there. It's become a duty that I perform for him, and he doesn't seem to think that it's very special either. How on earth could two people change so much so quickly?

Because Roger heard this story so often, when a couple comes to him for premarital counseling, he would ask them to agree to refrain from sexual intercourse until their wedding night. If they refused, he would tell them there was no way they could realistically prepare for marriage, and he gave them three reasons why.

God forbids sexual union outside of marriage. When a couple chooses to ignore God, they're starting their life together in a pattern of disobedience, so He won't help them establish the closeness for which they long. Clear consciences between them and God is destroyed.

Focusing your relationship on sex may keep you from finding true intimacy. We call sex "intimate," but that isn't necessarily so. Real intimacy is a deep and total sharing of your inner self—your joys and woes and hopes and griefs—with another.

Hillerstrom says, "To be intimate with a person is to be open, vulnerable, emotionally exposed, and trusting. But sexual intercourse can occur without any of that!" It's possible to have sex with a total stranger and to feel, for a moment, a surge somewhat akin to intimacy that isn't real intimacy at all. The truth is, if there's tension in a couples' relationship, it's possible for them to *avoid* working it out by simply hopping into bed. They leave their sexual union feeling great about each other for a little while, but the real issues between them have only been covered up, not healed. In time these festering sores will erupt into gaping, ugly wounds.

When a couple is sexually involved before marriage, they prepare themselves to feel sexual satisfaction only in illicit situations. It's like this. Something deep inside each person engaged in premarital sex says, "We shouldn't be doing this." And that's what makes it exciting. There is something definitely stimulating in the wrongness of the act. That illicitness is part of what brings sexual arousal, and both people are conditioning themselves to require it. After the wedding—*poof!*—what was once illegal is now perfectly legal and even expected. When it's not wrong, it's no longer fun. So how do these two find sexual excitement again? With an affair, of course. Bingo! Great sex again, but only so long as it remains illicit. What a trap to be caught in![2]

We could add a couple of other problems we've seen emerge from premarital involvement. For one thing, it opens the door to the *destruction of trust.* One couple who lived together for several months before their marriage finally divorced over the issue of trust. The wife said, "I remember how easy it was to get him into bed with me, and I can't get it out of my mind that another woman could get him just as easily as I did." She probably has a point. If a man and woman don't respect the marriage commitment enough to honor its boundaries before they marry, what's to guarantee they'll suddenly change just because they've walked down the aisle of a church?

Real love can *wait,* but lust has to have what it wants *right now.* Couples sexually involved outside of marriage have begun their life together on a basis of lust, not love. And lust isn't a force strong enough to keep a couple together for life. Marriage isn't a cure for lust, and where lust is present, the seeds of *disrespect* are able to root and grow.

Perhaps as you've read this you're thinking back to your own courtship. If you were involved sexually before your marriage, you may be feeling great guilt or despair as you understand the gravity of what you've done. If that's true, I come to you with words of hope. God convicts us of our sin so we will repent and go to Him. And then He will cleanse and heal us. The God we serve is not only Creator; He is also the Re-Creator. He can take your marriage and bring it to a state of purity before Him so that you can create a solid foundation for your lives together.

When Annie and I talk with couples who've sinned by engaging in premarital sex, we have them take each other's hand and pray something like this:

> *Father, we admit our wrongdoing. We have sinned against You and each other. Please forgive us. Cleanse us from our*

wrongs and the guilt we rightly feel. In Your mercy, help us begin anew right now, starting life together on the strong foundation of purity in You. We commit ourselves to each other completely and exclusively for the rest of our lives. We look to You, Lord, for the grace to keep this commitment until death parts us. Amen.

When you ask God to forgive you, He does (1 John 1:9)! He also promises to make you as pure before Him as if you'd never sinned in the first place (Isaiah 1:18).

Past Involvements Before Marriage

About six months after we were married, Annie ran into a friend who'd also married about the time we did. When Annie asked how their married life was going, the woman admitted she was bored. Married only six months and bored *already*? The woman went on to explain that she'd been involved with a number of other men before she married Tom, and her husband hadn't turned out to be quite as sexually exciting as some of the others.

It's now many years later, and with much effort this couple has survived their rocky beginning, and they've gone on to serve Christ. But they made it only by going through honest confession to the Lord and experiencing His cleansing of the past.

In an article years ago in *Ministry Today*, Richard Dobbins offered a great analogy. He said, sexuality is a lot like adhesive tape. It's not made to be used over and over. The strongest bond adhesive tape can form is with the first surface it sticks to. Of course, you can pull off a piece of tape and reapply it to other surfaces a number of times and it will still stick. But every time you do, it loses some of its ability to bond...until it finally won't stick to anything. Dobbins explained it this way: "Sexuality and bonding are inseparable. We cannot express ourselves sexually without affecting the bonding ability of our bodies." [3]

Sexual liaisons with anyone other than your spouse will only have bad repercussions. Even if the experience was good, it creates the problem Annie's friend had: a longing for someone other than her mate. If the experience was bad, it may leave you with negative feelings about sex that may cause issues in your marriage or be targeted toward your marriage partner.

Again, there can be cleansing and healing if you go to Christ and admit your wrong and ask for His forgiveness and healing. After David had sinned with Bathsheba, he went to God: "Have mercy on me, O God, according to your unfailing love; according to your great compassion blot out my transgressions. Wash away all my iniquity and cleanse me from my sin" (Psalm 51:1-2 NIV).

I'm not recommending that you sit down with your mate and rehearse the details of any pre- or extramarital encounters you may have had with others. Access to this kind of information gives Satan all kinds of weapons with which to torment your mate with fears, doubts, and bitterness. If you've confessed to the Lord and still feel uncertain where you stand, talk to a trusted Christian friend or spiritual advisor. Accept Christ's forgiveness and cleansing, and then go forth as David did, expecting to experience the joy of unhindered fellowship with the Lord and the ability to give yourself freely and fully to your mate.

Sexual Involvement Outside Your Marriage

I was saddened to hear that an old friend of mine had left his wife and three children for another woman. Annie and I had spent a lot time with this couple, and we never dreamed the husband would ever cross the line from faithful partner to dishonorable adulterer. In deciding to forsake his family, he lost his standing in the church, his reputation was demolished, his business was damaged, his parents' hearts were broken, and his wife and children were devastated.

What I couldn't figure out was how such a thing could happen when, in my opinion, he had such a lovely wife. What in the world could have enticed him into an affair with another woman, who, when I saw her, wasn't really that attractive? What was it about her that drew him away? Those questions were eventually answered, and I felt compelled to put them in a song to help others avoid the same downfall.

Easy to Steal

His wife was beautiful
She had a face to die for
Why he walked out her door
Who knows

And the woman he's with now
Everybody's saying she's a step down
But she won his heart somehow
And it shows

But then I heard it from a good friend
What she did to get to him
She didn't touch him with her hands
She just whispered in his ear

I guess it's true
It's not just how she looks
It's how she makes him feel
And she knew
If she used the right words
She could turn his wheel
The truth of the matter?
The one who can be flattered
Is easy to steal

She told him he was a good man
She told him she was his biggest fan
It wasn't new, but it was something
That he needed to hear [4]

Married but Not Dead

Just because you've made a sexual commitment to your spouse doesn't necessarily mean you'll never feel a twinge of attraction toward anyone else. In these times when sexual temptations have saturated our world, Annie and I have established some guidelines to help us stay true to the Lord and to each other:

- *Three are better than two.* Whenever one of us is meeting, traveling, or dining with a person of the opposite sex, we always make sure a third person is included. If there is an unavoidable change of plans, we let each other know right away.

- *Better safe than sorry.* We keep physical contact with other people to a minimum. A quick handshake or side-hug when greeting someone is fine, but loving embraces are reserved for relatives and dear friends. And even then, when it involves friends of the opposite sex, embraces are included only when others are present.

- *Words have meaning.* We keep our comments about others impersonal (observational). Commenting on the appearance of a person of the opposite sex may seem innocent enough at the time, but the words may be misunderstood or misinterpreted. Saying a person's outfit is pretty is quite different than saying the person looks beautiful.

- *Avoid the appearance of evil.* We do not use or condone suggestive comments, jokes, or gestures. Comments about sexuality and sexual conduct are always inappropriate and unnecessary.

- *Run for the hills!* If we sense an attraction or even a hint of temptation when with someone, we immediately leave the situation or make sure someone else is *always* present if that person can't be avoided. The same holds true if someone is being flirtatious or making inappropriate contact with us.

- *The spouse always gets a veto vote.* If one of us senses that a person isn't the kind of company the other should be keeping or spending time with, we listen and take the steps necessary to end the association. (This guideline may seem severe, but it has served us well.)

We established these rules years ago, and we are glad we did! We urge you to consider them as a base for determining your own rules of conduct to keep your marriage secure and your relationship with others above reproach. After all, when you value what you have, you do whatever it takes to protect it!

Preventative actions such as these leave no room at all for dabbling in pornography or sexually provocative movies. You want to avoid anything that makes sex less than the wonderful gift of God it is and suggests that someone besides your mate would better meet your emotional or physical needs.

Keeping a sexual commitment involves more than just what you *don't* do. Following Christ isn't just adhering to a bunch of don'ts. Rather, it's a holy adventure focused on what you *do* with Him and for Him and through Him. And we believe this is just as true for faithfulness in marriage. Staying faithful doesn't involve just not sleeping with someone other than your spouse. It means putting your best effort and energy into enhancing the romance you have with your mate. Faithfulness is more than just saying no to others; it's also saying yes to your spouse.

The Joys of Second Honeymoons

One of my favorite ways to keep on saying yes to this woman God has given me is to plan second honeymoons. This tradition began during a particularly difficult time in our life together. I was still on the road with the band, and we seemed to never have the time together we needed. I loved Annie, and I wanted a special way to show her how much. Thus was born the idea for a second honeymoon.

I secretly arranged for my mother to keep Nathan and Heidi for a weekend. I made a reservation at a motel out of town. Later Annie told me that weekend marked a turning point in our life together! When she saw the effort I took, she was convinced in an even deeper way of my love for her.

That second honeymoon turned out to be the first of many, and through experience (and the experiences of other couples who've tried it, as well), I've come up with some suggestions to help you create some second honeymoons of your own. Although these instructions are for husbands, they can be adapted for wives who want to plan second honeymoons.

I suggest the husband take the initiative in planning the second honeymoon. Women usually seem to be quicker to understand the need for time alone together, so be prepared to pick your wife up off the floor after she faints when you announce what you've planned.

If you want the weekend to be a surprise (and that makes it more fun), *you'll need to sneakily find out if the date you've chosen is clear on her schedule.* You may need to enlist the help of one of her friends to make sure the calendar date stays open. Also, you'll want to avoid the time of her monthly period. And if you want to display an incredible amount of sacrifice, plan your second honeymoon on either Super Bowl weekend, the start of the World Series, or during the NBA playoffs—and don't watch them, talk about them, or sneak a peak at a television.

If you have children, you'll need a sitter. Never call a prospective sitter and say, "You wouldn't want to keep my kids for 36 hours, would you? I probably shouldn't have asked…oh, never mind!" Instead, be honest and positive. Ask the potential sitter if she would be willing to take your kids so your wife and you can have some special, much-needed time together. The price you have to pay for a sitter will vary according to your time away and number of kids you have. Tell the sitter up front what you plan to pay to avoid any confusion. The sitter should know ahead of time what reward he or she can expect for such bravery. Also make sure she knows this is a surprise for your wife.

Most important: Make sure the sitter is dependable. Neither you nor your wife wants to be worrying about the kids while you're away. Leave the number of your place of lodging with the sitter, but also give strict instructions *not to call* unless she's being tied to a post and the kids are lighting matches.

I recommend staying at a motel. Why? A motel is usually more romantic and the two of you won't have to clean it when you leave (like you would if, for example, you stayed at a friend's cabin). Choose a place that's not more than one to three hours away. After all, who wants to spend the whole weekend driving? You might even want to go back to the same place you spent your first honeymoon. If you do, why not request the same room? Make sure you get a confirmation number. Sometimes motel clerks are forgetful, and you don't want to arrive and find your room has someone else in it.

Call a florist and arrange for flowers to be placed in your room. Be sure the message you ask to include with the bouquet sets a romantic tone for your time together. And when you pack, include a nice, fragrant candle. (It'll not only sweeten the air in your room, but the candlelight does wonders for untanned, wrinkled, and cellulite-dimpled bodies.)

When you arrive, take each other's hands and pray. Ask the Lord to purify the room and fill it with His love and protection.

Don't talk about the kids. This time is meant to remind you that you are not only Mom and Dad, you are also husband and wife, lovers, and friends. Avoid talking about business and all that other daily-life junk that fills up space but doesn't draw you closer. You're alone with a woman you're out to attract, impress, and enjoy. There'll be time to solve the problems with the plumber's bill and Johnny's math grade when you get home.

Plan entertainment that is fun for both of you. Don't get tickets to a ball game unless she's a big fan. Generally, do nothing that will make her feel as if she's just tagging along on your hobby weekend. Avoid movie theaters and plays because you'll wind up spending three hours watching other people relate to each other rather than getting closer yourselves. Especially avoid the television. If you wanted to spend your time with *Seinfeld* reruns, you should have saved your money, and stayed home.

Be full of surprises. Try writing her a poem and stashing it in her luggage when she's not looking. Buy a card that expresses how you feel about her. Get her some of her favorite perfume or bring along a music player with her favorite songs.

Plan at least one nice meal in a romantic restaurant. (If you're like me, you'll need to pray for grace to refrain from asking the manager to turn up the lights so you can see what you're eating.) For the weekend, you might also want to take along some snacks, such as grapes, cheese, and crackers. (If all goes well, you may find you never want to leave your room! You didn't on your first honeymoon, did you?)

As I mentioned, these instructions were aimed at husbands. However, I know that some women might wait a lifetime for their husbands to pull off a romantic getaway. If that's true for you, then certainly feel free to initiate second honeymoons. Maybe you can plan it together? However it happens, the rewards are worth it.

Speaking of Rewards

I know a husband who for more than six decades treated his bride in such a special way that he earned the greatest title any husband can ever be called. I personally heard his wife bestow this coveted title on him at their fiftieth wedding anniversary. What he was called by his sweet and very contented wife is the very title I long to receive when I reach the milestone with Annie that this seasoned couple did. If I hear her say about me what was said about that man, I know I'll have been successful as a husband. Here's a lyric I wrote about that husband and his coveted reward. And, by the way, the husband I'm referring to is none other than my dad, P.J. Chapman.

Has Been...

Mama stood up at the party
She said, "Fifty years ago
I married me this mighty fine man
And I want everybody to know..."
Then she smiled as she raised her glass
And said as she looked at him
"When it comes to great lovers
He's a 'has been'"

He has been faithful
He has been true
Whatever I wanted
He always came through
When I needed a lover
When I needed a friend
Through all these years
That's what he has been

Well, Daddy got a standing ovation
And we all got tears in our eyes
Then I looked at the ring on my finger
That's when I realized
I want to do it right like he did
I want to turn out just like him
So I can hear those words
Mama said about Daddy
"He's a has been" [5]

Customized Love

by Annie

Today so many people have become infatuated with personalizing their lives. It starts innocently enough. We engraved our initials on jewelry, stitched them onto sweaters, or etched them on crystal. But from this humble beginning, a massive industry devoted to personalization has grown. Stationery, key rings, mugs, and T-shirts all come emblazoned with your name. Your home can be resplendent with welcome mats, mailboxes, table linens, and Christmas ornaments bearing your insignia. Your kids can sport personalized schoolbags and swim-team jackets. They can read storybooks with their own names printed into the text. Every other computer-generated advertising letter stuffed in your mailbox uses your name more times than your mother does when she writes to you.

In the heat of this passion to personalize our world, we have overlooked the most important facet of our lives. We've failed to personalize the way we say "I love you."

Breaking Away from Generic Love

When we were first married, I heard a message from a lady in California who claimed to know all about "wife-ing." If a woman loved her husband, this woman insisted, she'd fix him breakfast in bed. Until then, Steve and I had eaten all our meals in an upright position, but I was anxious to do well at loving my man, so breakfast in bed it would be. Unfortunately, Steve didn't respond well to this innovation. California husbands must have some inbred athletic prowess he lacks because juggling that tiny little tray on his knees as he tried to keep from seeding the sheets with biscuit crumbs was too much to handle.

But I was determined to show I loved him. The next suggestion I came across in one of those "keeping the sizzle in your marriage" books insisted on candlelight dinners as the key to bliss. So the lights went down, and the candles were ignited. But Steve had a bad experience once with food he couldn't see, so he associated candlelight with nausea rather than passion. He's since gotten over this aversion, but at the time my idea was a flop. Once again I felt like a failure at romance.

After the candlelight fiasco, I came to a new conclusion. Perhaps these well-meaning teachers spoke so highly of these expressions of love because they'd married men who liked to eat in strange places. Maybe the secret to their success was not the bedside breakfasts, but rather that they'd studied their husbands long enough to know their likes and dislikes. What a new thought!

Spurred on by these conclusions, I started a study of Steve to find out how *he* liked to hear "I love you." Some of the answers I came up with proved to be unconventional, at best.

Love Means Scratching the "Sock Ridges"

Steve was born with inordinately large calves. I assume that when God designed him, He planned them as an asset to a boy from West Virginia who'd spend untold hours trudging up and down those Appalachian hills. But having calves shaped like upside-down bowling pins has its drawbacks. For one thing, his socks slide down as fast as he can pull them up, so when he jogs, he's had to resort to wearing socks with a thick elastic band around the top. Though they don't sag, the elastic also carves grooves around his ankles that feel miserable.

When he comes in from a hard run, he claims there's no experience closer to heaven than getting those ridges in his ankles scratched. In my study of Steve, I took note of this quirk and appointed myself "Official Ankle-Ridge Itch Remover." When he strips off his sweat socks, I invite him to plunk his feet in my lap. I scratch those ridges while he lies there on the floor with his tongue hanging out like a dog in ecstasy.

I'm willing to bet you've never read a marriage book that recommends ankle-scratching as a way to express your love to your mate! And you're not reading it now either. This particular way to say "I love you" does wonders for our married life because it's *tailored to us.*

Nongeneric Love Works for Men Too

My creativity pushed Steve to take a look at his adeptness as a lover. Did he love me? Of course he did, and in the general expressions of love, he was doing great. He'd married me, hadn't he? And forsaken all others for me…and hustled to earn a living so he could provide for me. Steve thanked me for cooking dinner and kissed me goodbye whenever he left the house.

But what I needed was to have that generic love *personalized.* I wanted him to find my "ankle ridges" too. So Steve started a study of his own. He discovered a secret to loving me that came at the kids' bedtime. After a long day, I can be short on the energy it takes to oversee the baths, the teeth-brushing, the storytelling, and the tucking-in that two active kids require. On those days, if he offers to take over pajama duty his action shouts "I love you" more loudly than dozens of roses ever could.

In your case, perhaps flowers delight your wife. Or what if you chose your wife's companionship over attending a sports event? Sometimes personalized love does mean presents; other times it means giving *your presence* in a special way.

How Do I Love Thee? Let Me Find the Ways!

Have you seen books that offer 1001 ways to love your spouse? If you've been tempted to buy one, the suggestion I'm about to offer will save you the trouble and $15.95. You don't need 1001 ways to love your spouse. More than likely, 945 of them won't mean much to your mate anyway. Just sit down with your partner and ask, "What would you like me to give you or do for you to let you know how much I love you?" Getting answers to this question will not only enhance your life together, it can save you much pain—as the Carters discovered.

Even though Tim and Barbara had just moved into a beautiful new home, there was no time to relax together in front of the magnificent stone fireplace or enjoy lazy Saturdays by the pool. Tim was never home. Finally, Barbara could take it no more.

"I feel as if you don't love me because you're working all the time," she told him through her tears.

Tim looked bewildered. "I was working so much *because* I love you. I wanted you to have the house you've always talked about. But I can't afford the payments without all this extra overtime. I don't like being gone so much, but I did it because pleasing you matters to me."

Tim believed money equaled love because of what he'd seen in his parents' marriage. His mother saw affection in high-priced gifts. Tim figured his wife held the same values. His incorrect assumption needlessly turned an act of love into a source of contention.

How does your mate need to hear "I love you"? Have you asked? Have you studied your spouse to find the answers for yourself? Steve's dad did. He studied his wife. That's why I can remember Steve's mother saying, "The carpet in this room has been easy to keep clean because Steve's father has always left his shoes on the porch when he comes home from the factory." He had the good sense to study his woman and find out what said love to her. I want to do the same. I want to become a "Steveologist"—to be so thoroughly in touch with this man I live with that he never lacks for love given in the form he wants it most.

Sometimes I'm motivated to this kind of giving from my great love for Steve, but other times I do it simply because I'm a reasonable woman. We two Chapmans have promised to be together until death parts us, right? Since we are making the journey together, why not be as happy as we can along the way? From my feminine viewpoint, I see romance this way. Most men provide adequately, work hard, and don't beat their wives. But most, it seems, are also what we would call unromantic. When we plan a nice meal and light the candles, we can count on them to ask if the electricity has been turned off.

Many guys have been taught from childhood that romantic means being sentimental and syrupy sweet—in other words, anything but manly. Perhaps your man's aversion to romance was even appealing to you when you were dating. Maybe that coolheaded objectivity and macho image he portrayed felt exciting to you. But now you miss the romantic niceties, and you're not sure your man is capable of change. So where does this leave you? It seems to me you have several choices, each with its own set of results.

- You can spend the rest of your married life resenting the man God has given you and become an expert at pity-party planning.

- You can dedicate the remainder of your earthly days to becoming the world's greatest nag, thus making your husband miserable.

- You can decide to suffer in silence, making yourself miserable.

- You can submit your married life to God's care and decide to dwell on your husband's good qualities. Then you can do all you can to create an atmosphere of love and warmth in your home.

I like that fourth option myself, and my husband does too. We're determined to stick together, so we've decided to make our marriage the best it can be. And you know, finding those special ways to please each other has made the trip a lot more fun!

When Memories Turn to Gold

We made another memory today
We thought it was beautiful
Someone else may look and say
"Why, it's nothing so unusual."
But someday they will turn to gold
These memories we gather
So there's a reason we must hold
Tightly to these treasures

'Cause we're holding on to something
Only two can share
And when no one else can touch them
That makes them rich and rare
And someday when we sit and spin
These yarns inside our souls
For you and me that will be
When our memories turn to gold

So one by one we'll gather them,
Memories for our winter

They'll warm our hearts someday when
Our days are cold and bitter

'Cause we're holding on to something
Only two can share
And when no one else can touch them
That makes them rich and rare
And someday when we sit and spin
These yarns inside our soul
For you and me, that will be
When our memories turn to gold[1]

Staying Tuned-In

Personalized love isn't static, so don't expect to sit down with your spouse one day to cement in place a lifetime list of ways you can best give your love. If you're doing things right in your marriage, both of you are going to change and grow. In Ephesians 5:29, God, through the apostle Paul, tells husbands to nourish their wives. When we nourish our tomatoes with plant food, they grow. When we nourish our kids with Wheaties, they get bigger. And when Steve provides emotional food to satisfy my "soul hunger," I grow too. With growth comes change. As I grow, Steve will listen for the new ways I want to hear "I love you." The same holds true for husbands. As I respect and complete Steve, he grows. My expressions of love for him need to adjust to the man he's becoming.

One woman I know reflected on these changes as she talked about the computer her husband had given her for her birthday:

> When we first married, if he'd have given me an expensive machine I'd have been furious. I was terribly uncertain about my own womanliness, so a gift like this would

have confirmed my worst fears. It would have labeled me businesslike and competent…in other words, a workhorse. I would have seen it as an appropriate gift for a business partner, but not something he would give to his betrothed. So for those early birthdays he came through with perfume and outrageous, lacy things and other tangible evidences that assured me I was attractive to him.

Now it's [many] years later, and I'm much more sure of my femininity. I've begun to dream some professional dreams I didn't have before. For instance, I'm taking steps to turn my interest in accounting into a legitimate business. My husband let me know he sees and supports how I've changed by investing a sizable chunk of money in a data-processing setup for me. When I protested about the cost, he waved me off. "You can't do your work without the right tools," he said. Do you see why I continue to be so crazy about this man?

If Your Partner Doesn't Personalize His Love

What a pleasure when you've worked hard to see love as your mate does, and he or she returns the favor. When both of you give— and *get*—you find marital oneness at its best. But what about when the giving seems one-sided? What then?

You can teach your mate the ways you'd like to receive love. Just as some people take more naturally to ice skating, or songwriting, or cooking, some of us have built-in relational capacities others lack. In marriage, it's common to find couples in which a "relater" pairs with a "nonrelater." Your spouse may suffer from dulled nerve endings when it comes to picking up your vibrations. Maybe your spouse doesn't personalize love because he or she just plain can't figure out what you need or desire.

You may need to be the teacher, studying yourself to find out which love expressions mean most and then passing on your observations to your partner. Don't be discouraged if it takes more than one 10-minute talk to communicate what you mean.

From the beginning of our marriage, I've always been very verbal. If I felt Steve hadn't been giving me enough attention, I'd say, "Steve, I need more attention." I made the directions simple and straightforward. "Steve, I need you to tell me you love me." Or "Steve, tell me I'm pretty." Or "Steve, tell me I'm your best friend." After he'd accommodate me, I'd thank him and go on with my business, content because I knew that even though I prompted him, he meant what he said.

You may not think a compliment is worth much if you have to ask for it. In times past, I would have agreed with you. But finally it occurred to me that my husband couldn't read my mind. If he were going to meet my needs, he'd have to know what those needs were. The book of Proverbs teaches that "a man dies from lack of instruction" (5:23). I believe a relationship can die while you wait for your partner to learn to read your mind and understand your needs.

Some people are easier to teach than others. One woman we know realized she needed her husband's love to come in the form of what she called "affection when the lights are on." She wanted him to hold her hand as they walked together, or put his arm around her as they watched television, or catch her eye at a church supper in one of those "you're mine and I'm glad" kind of glances they gave each other during their courtship. "He's tender and affectionate when the lights are out," she said. "But when the daylight comes, he freezes." This woman isn't unique in her desire. We need eight to ten meaningful touches each day to maintain physical and emotional health. [2] And the majority of a woman's desire for meaningful touch is nonsexual.

Though she mentioned these desires to her husband several times, he'd always mumble something about "not being a very touchy person." And nothing changed. Then, during one particularly intimate moment, she approached the topic again. But this time she took a tack he understood. "I explained to him that not having this day-time affection was as devastating to me as it would be for him if we gave up making love. *That was a message he could grasp.* And though he'll never need all the hugs and squeezes I do, he's now working harder to become more 'touchy,' as he calls it. It just took time and the right moment to help him understand what I was saying."

You can appreciate the love your partner does have to give. Some husbands or wives feel unloved even when it's not true. Their mates do, in fact, love them and show it, but the partners refuse to read the love signs as they're posted. For instance, a woman may wish her husband would "say it with flowers," and indeed he should, since that's how she wants to hear love. But to accuse him of not loving her because he doesn't show love that way may be unfair. Perhaps he's revealing his love when he spends a Saturday wallpapering the family room because she wants to change the color scheme. He'd rather be golfing, but for love for his wife, he chooses paste over a putter.

Although we want to personalize our love and have love personalized for us, at the same time, let's not reject the pleasure of the love we're offered even if it isn't packaged the way we'd prefer.

You can give personalized love anyway. Your mate may need long-term exposure to examples of personalized love before he or she gets the idea. Jesus took this approach with us. Perhaps your story is like mine. Christ wooed me for years before I responded to Him. How glad I am He didn't give up when I didn't respond quickly! Because He patiently and persistently gives Himself to us, you and I can give to our mates without instant returns.

So go ahead. Pass your spouse the generic raisin bran or offer a cup of generic coffee. But when it comes to loving, don't settle for generalities. Make your caring personally tailored to the one you love. For another example of a husband who follows this advice, consider the gentleman who discovered a way to personalize his expression of love for his wife by inviting her to do something with him that he typically enjoyed doing alone. We put his excellent (and cost free) suggestion in this lyric.

Come and Walk with Me

Come and walk with me
We'll talk and reminisce
About the places we have been
And old friends we miss
We'll spend some steps together
Make a back-road memory
Underneath that big, blue sky
Come and walk with me

Come and walk with me
We'll talk about today
And the things that make us weary
And the dreams that keep us awake
For a while we'll let our burdens
Be carried by the breeze
Let the songbirds serenade us
Come and walk with me

Come and walk with me
We'll talk about tomorrow
And where we'd like to go
In the rest of the days we borrow
And by the time we turn around
At that old willow tree
There'll be no distance between our hearts
Come and walk with me [3]

10

The Ships Are Burning...

by Steve

*I*f there's nothing in your life you'd be willing to die for, then you don't have anything to live for either. What I'm talking about is commitment. It's what Jesus talked about when He told the story of a man who found a valuable pearl in a field. The man went at once and sold everything he had to buy the field so the pearl could be his. If the pearl later turned out to be worthless, he'd be left with nothing because he risked all he had to own it.

Commitment. It's what the Spanish explorer Cortes insisted on when he landed in Mexico. When he saw his crew's fear and vacillation about invading the land, Cortes gathered them all on shore and then set fire to the vessels on which they'd come. Now there could be no turning back! They were committed to going forward.

Commitment is a man and woman standing together before God and His people and pledging to forsake all others and cleave only to each other until death—and only death—parts them. Or at least that's what marriage was meant to be. God created it to show a watching world the loving, exclusive, permanent union of Jesus Christ with His people.

But people of today decided to remake marriage to suit their convenience. They decided the "exclusive" stuff was too much trouble, so they came up with and promoted an "open marriage." When we understand the deep and eternal bonding that happens between two people when they marry before God, we can laugh at how ridiculous it is to combine the concept of "open" and the concept of "marriage" together in one phrase. It makes about as much sense as trying to talk about a humble politician or a jumbo shrimp. Marriage is a commitment before God, and representative of Jesus' love for the church (His followers). Marriage can't be "open" and still be a marriage by definition.

Instead of keeping marriage a permanent union, people decided it should last "only as long as our love [the gushy feelings, the chemistry] lasts." Sticking together without a tidal wave of feelings to carry them has become almost unthinkable.

One Christian man showed this belief when he shared, "I married her at 18, and right then we seemed like a great fit. In the years after, we both changed so much we no longer made each other happy. Surely no one expects me to have to be chained for a lifetime to the immature choice I made as a teenager."

Love is what draws you together, but it is not the basis for marriage. Marriage is a covenant you made to your spouse before God. It holds true regardless of how we feel. Emotions can be fickle at best. Hopefully we've been helping you discover how to keep your mate's cup filled up with love. But if the days come when he or she isn't filling your cup, those will be the moments to go back to the commitment you made and ask God to help you keep it and help you rediscover your first love.

The Ships Are Burning

We made this journey; we sailed here together
We made a promise; we'd stay here forever
And when we reached the shore, we kissed the ground
You took my hand, and we turned around
And we smiled as we watched the flames
Light up the night

'Cause the ships are burning
There'll be no turning back for you and me
Whatever we find here, we've made it clear
Here is where we'll always be
And on this island of pleasure, there'll be some dangers
And we might think about returning
But we both know we won't go—that's why
The ships are burning

But too many lovers
Are keeping their ships anchored in the bay
One by lonely one we've seen them sail away
But when we reached the shore, we kissed the ground
You took my hand, and we turned around
And we smiled as we watched the flames
Light up the night[1]

Another reason to remember your commitment are your children (if you have them). Divorce has become such an easy part of our world that most people gloss over the vast devastation it wreaks on children when their parents divorce. Studies and statistics regarding children of divorced parents are one thing. It's another to have those children on your block so you often see the pain in their eyes. Years ago we took a couple of the neighborhood kids whose parents were divorcing with us to the gym for the evening. On the way, these kids described to ours what it was like living in a home where everything they counted on was falling down around them.

The little girl told of her mother's crying and screaming, of her daddy who closed his ears to it all, and of seeing everything she owned thrown into cardboard boxes to be taken off to a strange apartment. My heart broke for these two helpless victims of the cruelest of wars—a war in which there are no heroes and no winners—just wounded, hurting casualties on every side.

Besides your children, there's another, even more powerful reason to keep on with your marriage commitment despite the toughest of times. That reason? God hates divorce (Malachi 2:16). (And if you've been through this havoc or are close to someone who has, you understand why.) So your desire to honor and obey Him can help pull you toward keeping your marriage vows even if your partner hasn't.

If your marriage is in trouble, fight for it with all that's within you. Exhaust every available opportunity to make the marriage work. I talked to a couple who had been married 39 years. They'd been through some stormy times, but in their tenth year of marriage came the bout to end all bouts. The wife got so mad she pulled her suitcase out of the bedroom closet and started packing.

"What are you doing?" her husband demanded.

"I'm leaving."

Without a word he got out his suitcase and started filling it with his clothes.

"Now what are *you* doing?" his wife asked.

"If you're leaving," he told her firmly, "I'm going with you."

There was a man determined to do what it took to keep his marriage together. And sheer determination is sometimes what it takes. You may be feeling right now that you've lost the determination or will to fight, but be sure of this: If you choose to fight on behalf of your family, God will respond to you. Your commitment to Him will move Him to marshal His power and grace on your behalf and on behalf of your family. When you choose to follow Christ even though the price might seem overwhelming, Christ commits to being with you. "If anyone serves Me, the Father will honor him" (John 12:26).

Of course, we all know every story doesn't turn out the way we want it to. Maybe that's what happened in your marriage. Even though you were committed, faithful, and determined to preserve your home, your spouse was not. It is true that God has given each of us free will, and sometimes people use their free will to do some destructive and sad things. As a result of a spouse's choice, you may have been left with a broken heart and a shattered family.

God has not forgotten you! He is more than willing and able to be a divine shoulder you can lean on. Grab His heavenly hand and allow Him to comfort you. In the same way Jesus Christ is here to help keep a family together, He is also here to take the broken pieces in our lives and create a beautiful mosaic. God's ultimate plan for your life is not dependent on the whims and whys of another person.

While my words can't restore your home, God can heal it. Through His Word, He reminds you that…

- He loves you (1 John 4:19).

- He is in control (Romans 8:28).

- You can trust Him (Proverbs 3:5-6).

Verbalize Your Commitment

From time to time, we need to put our commitment into words. I don't believe I had ever given my wife or children cause to wonder whether or not I'm going to give the rest of my life to loving them and serving them. But after that heart-wrenching episode in the car with our neighbor's children, Nathan said to me, "Daddy, is this going to happen to us? Are you going to leave us?"

If I hadn't been driving the car, I'd have taken that little boy in my arms, hugged him, and reassured him physically and verbally. Instead, I told him firmly, "Son, I am committed to your mother, to you, and to Heidi. I promised God a long time ago that I would stay in this family, and I will." Nathan said nothing for a moment, but I sensed even this clear affirmation wasn't yet enough.

"Promise?"

"Yes, son, I promise." I could see acceptance and certainty flood his face. *Whew!* Seeing how much my family needed this kind of confirmation has prompted me several times since to look for chances to make my commitment clear to them. More than once I've gathered my family near me and said, "Annie, I love you. I am going to stay with you regardless of what may happen." Then I turn to each of the children and restate my intentions to them. And then Annie commits herself to each of us as well. We end this special time with a prayer of thanks to God for His faithfulness even as we tell Him that we also promise to be faithful to *Him*.

There are two other things that help strengthen me to stand by my commitment. One is the encouragement of other believers who understand the importance of marriage and whose examples give me courage when I need to stick it out through the bad times. People like my parents who spent more than 65 years serving Christ and each other. People like Joe and Linda Goodman, Henry and Hazel Slaughter, Bob and Peggy Hughey, and countless others who have held high God's desire for marriage and taught us how to make His desires a reality. The other real resource of strength has been praying with Annie. Praying *for* her is one thing; praying *with* her is quite another. This was a grace and joy I needed to learn how to do effectively, but it's been well worth the effort.

One of the first times Annie and I tried this business of praying together happened back when we were dating. We were driving along in Sarah, that old '50 Chevy I told you about before. We were on our way to church one night in the rain when Sarah died. Or sort of died. She didn't lose engine power, but she wouldn't go forward anymore. I pulled off the road and came to a stop on the shoulder. I was steaming with frustration. I mumbled, "I'm gonna have to get out and walk in this rain. And that gas station is probably a mile back or more." I sputtered a few more complaints between clenched teeth.

Annie held out her hand to me and said sweetly, "Let's pray for Sarah."

When she made the suggestion, I got even more frustrated... mostly because she'd suggested it, which wounded my ego. (If she'd just given me another 45 minutes or so, I'm sure I would have come up with the idea.) I may have an ego, but I'm no fool. I realized right away I had two options. I either had to pray with Annie or get out and start walking in the rain. I took Annie's hand. To be honest, I'd never prayed for a car before. (Up to this time I'd never had to because I'd always driven Fords!) Even though my faith was weak, I bowed my head and prayed something like, "Oh, Master Mechanic, Sarah's sick. We don't know what's wrong with her, Lord, and we have to come to You because we don't know whom else to go to. We're on our way to church. Please heal Sarah. Lord, I've never prayed for a car before, but I believe all things are possible with You. Amen."

Well, I put the key back in old Sarah's ignition and started up the engine. It started fine, but that hadn't been the problem. The real test was still ahead. I pushed in the clutch, dropped her down into first gear, and gave her a little bit of gas. When I let out on the clutch, I mean to tell you I never felt a tighter chassis. That transmission took hold, and we hit the highway so smoothly I didn't even have time to look back.

I was driving down the road yelling, "*Wow!* A brand-new car! Lord, while You're at it, could You heal the play in this steering wheel?" My faith was so exuberant that if there'd been a dead man lying alongside the road I probably would've stopped and yelled, "Hey you—get up in Jesus' name!" All right, I got a little carried away. But some of us need more dramatic experiences than others to get us started.

In the years since, Annie and I have not consistently gotten such instantaneous and exciting results. We've had times when we've been praying in one direction and God has taken us in another. But the times Annie and I have spent in prayer have done more than anything else to bind us together within a love that's bigger than our own. Talking to God refuels us to serve each other out of love for Christ. And because of that service, our romance continues to grow and grow. We believe it because God's Word says so and because we've seen it and experienced it work in our life together.

Even with these resources—married believers who encourage us and the power of praying with Annie—I sometimes feel as if our marriage is a tiny outpost in the midst of enemy territory with enemy troops shooting at us from every side. These enemies include:

- *Time pressure.* The push to do it all and meet everyone's expectations. *Ka-boom!*

- Temptations, which include indulging in immoral thoughts or relationships or choosing money or success over God's plan for us. *Blam!*

- Trials from the wear-and-tear of life and the pain of those around us whose suffering touches us so deeply. *Pow!*

Somehow in the midst of this onslaught, these moments of recommitment strengthen and refocus me. I may do many things with my life, but if I fail my family nothing else matters as much. They are the pearl of great price, fully worth giving all I own.

In their powerful book *The Language of Love*, Gary Smalley and John Trent have an important message for those of us who are trying to live out God's plan for marriage in the face of all kinds of opposition. I'll let them tell in their own words the story of a man who found hope in a hopeless situation. The man you'll meet is a young Marine, the time is World War II and the place is the island of Iwo Jima.

> The date was February 21, 1945—two days after the landing. Jerry had taken cover in a small crater formed by an exploding artillery shell. The shelling from back in the mountains had kept everyone awake almost all night. The morning had dawned with falling rain and restless fog drifting in the distant, higher slopes. But when the skies cleared and the Japanese could pick out their targets, the artillery bursts were joined by small-arms fire.

> Jerry had already given up all hope of coming off the island alive. Of the fourteen men in his rifle section, only he and five others hadn't been wounded or killed. In just two days, he had already seen far too much death. But its cruel hand was just beginning to strike: More Marines would die on Iwo Jima than on all the other battlefields of World War II combined. So many had died or been wounded around him already that he felt he had as much chance of living as keeping a soap bubble from bursting in the wind.

> That's when his corporal crawled up next to him and flashed him a grin. "You still alive, Jerry?" he said in his southern accent, offering Jerry a swig from a priceless canteen of water. "We're gaining on them, you know."

"How do you know that?" Jerry answered back with a thin smile. "Nobody came running up to me with a white flag last night."

"Look here, son, I have it on good authority. Tomorrow you'll see our boys on top of that hill. We're going to make it." Then he looked up at the fog-tipped volcano and spoke the words Jerry has never forgotten: "You'll see the flag tomorrow."

From the time the Marines first sighted Iwo Jima from the decks of their ships, they had been looking up at the highest point on the island. It was the top of Mount Suribachi, an extinct volcano. It was only 550 feet high, but the way death rained down from its steep, ragged slopes, it seemed more like Mount Everest. To have the American flag up there would mean that—at least from this hill—death would have lost its frightening foothold. It would also be the best sight any Marine had seen since he had landed.

As events turned out, Jerry wouldn't see the flag for another two days. And his corporal would never see it. He was killed in action that night. But on February 23, 1945, the hill was taken.

As the Stars and Stripes flew above them for the first time, men all over the island stood and cheered, ignoring the risk of exposing their positions.

When Jerry saw the flag, the words his corporal had spoken came back in full force. And those same words would give him strength to carry on during the next eight days until he was critically wounded and carried off the island.

"When I got off Iwo alive, I felt my life had been given back to me," Jerry said. "You never forget something like that. In the years since, whenever I've had things go wrong I remember my corporal's words. When things look their toughest, I just think back and say to myself, 'Hang in there, Jerry. You'll see the flag tomorrow.'" [2]

If you're hanging on in the midst of a tough marriage, then let me encourage you that God will not forget you. You too will see the flag tomorrow. You can say with Solomon, "His banner over me is love!" (Song of Solomon 2:4).

Someone asked the French general Napoleon to explain his defeat at Waterloo. The British didn't win because they had a better trained army or because they were better equipped, he said. They weren't victorious because they had more soldiers. The British took the battle, Napoleon believed, because they fought five minutes longer.

Sometimes I wonder what battles we've lost because we stop fighting five minutes before the Lord is ready to raise the flag of victory. We so badly need to hold on to Him and to the commitments we've made. God will grace us with what we need to honor Him.

It's impossible for me to think of God's provision of grace without Linda and Mike coming to mind. This beautiful couple had it all. Linda was a former Miss Texas beauty pageant contestant, a concert pianist, and a deeply committed Christian. Mike loved Christ too. And because he came up in the oil business during the boom years, his career took off like a gusher. They had it all.

But Linda caught a virus, which inexplicably moved into the lining of her brain. Within days this vibrant young woman lay comatose in a hospital bed awaiting death.

By God's grace Linda survived, though doctors predicted she'd never be much more than a vegetable. She fought her way back and can now walk, although with a stiff-legged and unsteady gait. She can talk too, though her speech is slow and labored. As great as the miracle of her recovery is, the best miracle is the love God gave Mike for his wife. Just two weeks before Linda's illness struck, the Lord burdened Mike with a desire to grow deeper in his love for his wife. "Lord," Mike prayed, "let me love my wife as Christ loved the church." I believe God was graciously preparing Mike for what was to come, and with that prayer Mike was saying he was onboard. In less than 14 days, Mike would know what it meant to give himself in love to someone who had nothing at all to give back. How much more clearly could we picture the kind of love Christ has for us?

In the months following Linda's affliction, Mike needed to provide for her every need and was given little hope of seeing progress. Another man might have left—or stayed filled with resentment and self-pity. Instead, Mike radiates love for Linda. And not the Hollywood kind of meaningless mush that turns tail at the first hint of adversity. Mike shows a strong, giving love—the kind of love that Jesus portrayed when He chose to face the horror of the cross and count it all joy.

> Seeing their love is why—
> We believe a man and wife
> Would have a better married life
> If they would try out-serving one another.
>
> For deeper love is felt
> When what is done is not for self
> But when it's done to satisfy the other.

We pray God's blessings on you as you fan the home fires through your service to each other and to Christ.

11

Growing Together

by Annie

*S*teve and I have never had much success with sharing a regular Bible-reading and prayer time. As we've mentioned, we each read God's Word independently. Reading it together had never become a habit. However, after our kids got older, we felt a need to establish a regular time for our family to meet together for devotions.

Our children were less than enthusiastic. They could spend a whole evening watching *Little House on the Prairie* reruns with such intensity you'd think they were getting paid for it by the hour. But just let us mention it was time to read Scripture, and it was as though they'd both been instantly struck with a terminal case of sleeping sickness. Their yawning and stretching and complaining and groaning could have easily put them in the running for an Emmy nomination.

Steve grew up in a home where a "family altar" was as much a part of the daily routine as breakfast, so he especially was convinced we needed to get one going for ourselves. He and I decided we'd take a crack at reading enough verses each day to get through the Bible in a year.

As the year progressed, we did fairly well in fulfilling our goal. The only times that really discouraged us came when travel or concerts caused us to miss a few days so we'd have to play catch-up. What should have normally been a 10- to 15-minute session would then stretch to a 45- to 60- minute time of Bible reading.

And being the conscientious Christian that he is, Steve was never content to just drone out the words. He was determined we'd know the deep truths of each passage. To make sure we weren't letting our minds wander as he trudged us through some wilderness wandering in the book of Numbers, he'd pick a bleary-eyed moment and hit us with a pop quiz on what he'd just read aloud.

"Where did the children of Israel camp after they left Oboth?" he'd ask. If we failed to dredge up the correct answer, he'd threaten to start the day's reading all over again. The children and I lived in mortal fear that Steve would catch the glazed look in our eyes or glance up just as one of us let go a stifled yawn. When that happened, the guilty party was targeted for "The Question." (As we went along, Steve and I began to take turns reading. When it was my night to read, you can guess who consistently wound up on the hot seat trying to recall Bible information a theology professor would have struggled to come up with.)

Well, calendar pages turned, and so did the chapters of our Bible. By Christmas we found ourselves with the end in sight. That's why on Christmas Day Steve was determined we'd get our reading done *before* the gift explosion. My sister and her two-year-old son, Billy, were visiting us, so before Steve began reading I turned on the camcorder that was set up in the living room so we'd be able to treasure the memory of the beautiful tapestry of a loving family gathered to read Scripture before we shared our deep love through the giving of gifts.

Just before I turned on the camera, a thought occurred to me. "Steve," I sweetly inquired, "since it's Christmas, why don't we read the Christmas story instead of the assigned reading?" I didn't see this request as unreasonable because at the time we were somewhere deep in the Minor Prophets section of the Bible.

"That would be fine," he answered, "but if we do, we'll get behind and have to play catch-up."

Those words struck terror in all our hearts, so reluctantly we agreed to stick to the schedule.

Little Billy, however, decided majority did not rule. Before him sat a Mount Everest of presents, and he was ready to scale the heights. When his mother tried to explain about the great encouragement we were about to receive from the reading of God's Word, Billy let loose a barrage of protests that only a two-year-old could create. It didn't take long to realize he had no intention of quitting, so Steve plowed ahead into the Scripture. It worked out all right because the day's passage turned out to be one of those tension-filled Old Testament stories where children were being brutally slaughtered and their bodies dashed to pieces, where blood ran down the streets, and where women were having their guts reamed out with swords. With a scriptural scenario like that, Billy's thrashing and moaning seemed to blend right in and even provided appropriate sound effects.

By the time we hit the final verse, my exhausted sister was slumped on the sofa, sweaty from trying to control her little tiger. Billy had moved into uttering those low guttural gasps that hang on when a child has worn himself out with uncontrolled crying. My stomach was feeling as though dinner wasn't such a good idea after all, and our children were poised like runners at the starting block as they waited for an okay to go for the gifts.

The best part of the evening came when we realized we'd recorded this mayhem, sound and all. When I finally mustered up the nerve to watch this film of the "Chapman's Christmas Devotional Hour," it was as horrifying and hilarious as I imagined.

Well, we did persevere in our Bible reading, and on December 31 we held a major family celebration. We'd read through the entire Bible together! More importantly, we'd participated in an entire year of family devotions, and all survived. We even found we'd grown from it.

When we started up again on January 1, we changed the format a bit. We read from an easier-to-understand translation of the Bible and concentrated more on the New Testament. And we added a time of prayer together.

You may have the idea our year of discipline produced perfect family devotions, but it didn't. During one moment of spiritual insanity when the kids were quite small, Steve and I decided it would be more reverent if we gathered in a circle and got down on our knees to pray, bowing lowly before the Lord. But to our horror, the most unsavory thing started happening. You see, when the children folded their little bodies into a kneeling prayer position, the pressure on their tiny abdomens created an unexpected problem. They, uh…umm…how do I put this without being offensive? Well, let me simply say, I thought perhaps I needed to eliminate pinto beans from their diets. We let them know how irritated we were that they weren't exercising more control out of reverence for the Lord. Then Steve and I quickly disappeared into our bedroom to laugh uncontrollably into our pillows. God was on the kids' side. Steve and I realized we were putting a measure of pressure on our children that God never asked for, and if we were going to demand such a level of cooperation during devotions, we'd have to live with the side effects that came with it. We went back to sitting on the couch for our prayer time, and it worked much better.

If we learned anything from our ventures into communal spiritual growth, it's the value of sticking with it no matter what the interruptions or pull to do something else. The benefits didn't stop with the children either. Steve and I were often more encouraged and learned more from our time than the children. We wondered too if we would have had an easier time getting started with the kids if we'd established a regular devotional time as a couple before our children were born.

Of course, you and your spouse will need to find the best way for the two of you to share in spiritual growth. The late Charlie and Martha Shedd helped thousands of couples through their marriage seminars and books that offered timeless wisdom, including *Letters to Karen: On Keeping Love in Marriage*, and *Celebration in the Bedroom*. Like the rest of us, they had to work out their own method for doing devotions together. They talked about their struggle in an interview with the editors of *The Wittenburg Door*. Their story is best told in their own words:

> *Charlie:* [At the start of our marriage] we were becoming estranged from each other and we didn't want this estrangement. We decided to do something about it. We committed ourselves to (a) time with each other, (b) total honesty, (c) prayer. That's what we're really pushing for in marriage: prayer! If we can get a couple to commit themselves for a duet of prayer, they can build a good marriage. Once they begin relating to the Lord, their relationship grows in depth.
>
> If the two of you can't seem to pray together out loud, try what we did. We began our prayers in silence.
>
> *Martha:* We have a favorite place where we sit down—a rocking loveseat in our living room. We hold hands and talk over the things we want to pray about. Anything that is troubling us or something we're grateful for. Then we pray silently. We started this way, and we still do it. Anybody can do that. Then we say the Lord's Prayer or "Amen" when we think we've gotten through.
>
> *Charlie:* We have four goals at our house for a praying home.
>
> *Martha:* One goal is that each of us has a quiet time every day. Charlie and I get up early, and we have our quiet time…reading the Bible or inspirational books. This is our time of meditation. Another goal in our family

is that everybody prays for everybody else every day. (There are thirteen now, including in-laws and grandchildren.) Third, we pray together as husband and wife. And our final goal is family devotions. We try to do that every day, and we succeed most of the time, maybe seventy-five percent. It's a real celebration time.

Charlie: Back to the quiet time: Study is a big part of our prayer life. We study material together that we share with each other. Once in a while we read a book together. Martha reads to me or I read to her. We do this sometimes when we're in the car. But more often we read alone in our quiet time. We read the Bible. Then we discuss what we read. "I came on this verse, honey, and it said this to me. What do you think?"

Martha: We think discipline is all-important, but our prayer life isn't rigid. It's a relaxed discipline. And it's something we have a good time at—like our family devotions. [1]

The Shedds made their devotional time work because they found ways to adapt it to their needs and lifestyle. Sometimes people are reluctant to explore and experiment because of the guilt they feel for not making the traditional devotion time work for them. If I'm describing you, you'll be encouraged by Randy and Phyllis Michael's journey to find a meaningful way to share their spiritual life.

Phyllis shared, "Another week had gone by and we still had not had 'family devotions.' I felt guilty and condemned. How could God be pleased with us—a pastor and his wife unable to find time [for] reading together and praying? Interruptions or unexpected schedule changes often short-circuited our well-laid plans. The result: guilt feelings. Those little signs 'Ours Is a Family Altar Home' only added to my frustration. I had visions of everyone else happily gathered in loving, warm, family groups every day and having family devotions, while Randy and I remained spasmodic in our attempts."

Then one day Phyllis heard a Christian friend she admired confessing to struggles with family devotions. Phyllis suddenly felt less alone and more free to ask the Lord for a plan that might work in her life with Randy. She talked to Randy, and they decided to start right where they were. Since both already had a private time of Bible reading, they worked on making this more meaningful. Each continued to read a short passage daily and separately they answered questions about the passage according to a plan they call the "SMU Approach." "What does it *say*?" "What does it *mean*?" "How can I *use* it?" Then they planned three or four times a week when they would meet and share with each other what they were learning.

"For us it's been helpful to plan the week ahead on Sunday afternoon," Phyllis explained. "We mark on our calendars specific times for spiritual sharing, knowing that our plan is flexible. After each of us shares our discoveries from a particular passage, we talk together about the implications of the verses for us. Often we will pray together about what we've found in the Word as it relates to our needs. Finally, we make some commitment to action on the basis of the Word.

"Many times we experience a closeness during our sharing that spreads into other areas of our relationship. Our spirits commune, and we experience a sense of our potential as a Christian couple." [2]

Accountability

There's another side to shared spiritual growth that Steve and I value. Just as we're committed to support and encourage each other, we believe we're accountable to hold each other to high standards. Sometimes that's easy; other times it isn't.

I recall the time when we were first married and went out for a burger. I wanted onion rings, but instead of stating my request I slid over in the booth, snuggled up next to Steve, and in a little baby coo just dripping with come-on, I said, "Honey, could I have some onion rings?" I thought no man with an ounce of hormones in his veins could resist.

But Steve turned straight toward me and firmly replied, "No."
No? Had I heard my new groom correctly?

"Annie," he said, "you were trying to manipulate me to get your way, and that's not the right way for us to begin our life together."

I didn't speak to him for two days. But he was right. And how glad I've been in the years since that he expected me to act like the woman of God I want to be, even if holding me to God's standard cost him some peace at home.

And Steve's been faithful more than once. I remember the time we drove from Nashville to Chicago to fulfill a singing engagement. We'd been told to prepare a 45-minute presentation, but after we arrived, we found out the organizers hadn't organized so we wound up with five minutes instead. We'd driven six hours to sing two songs! I was steaming. As it turned out, we were given another opportunity to sing that night, but by concert time I was still furious. My beloved decided I was in no spiritual condition to minister to anyone; therefore, I wouldn't be singing with him! While he did the concert, I was banished to the van like a naughty schoolgirl sent off to the corner. Once again, he had to endure some moaning from me. But eventually I was reminded that I trust Steve because he believes I belong to God first and to him second.

And Steve expects me to hold him accountable as well. I had to take my turn the night we sang for a special gathering of program directors from a number of radio stations. Having these people like us would make a huge difference in our career, and we wanted to succeed like never before. Our passion to make a good impression left us both so nervous we could barely sing. Steve had such a case of cotton-mouth he felt as if someone had stuffed a T-shirt down his throat. And to make things worse, during our performance, we heard snickers and laughing in the audience. With a bright spotlight shining right in our eyes, we couldn't see the people in the first row, so we had no way of knowing the laughter was actually coming from a party next door. We assumed the audience was ridiculing our performance.

We left that stage as low as we'd ever been. We slunk off to a booth in the darkest corner of a restaurant to hide and lick our wounds.

Steve was heading into the third chorus of "Poor Me" when it hit me that we were displeasing the Lord. I stopped my husband in mid-whine. "Honey," I told him, "the Lord may have shown us great mercy by letting us fail so miserably. We wanted to impress those people and make a name for ourselves. If we'd accomplished that, we may have been on our way to becoming a public success but a disappointment in the eyes of God."

Steve didn't shower me with gratitude for these words of admonition. What he wanted at that moment was a pity partner. But he did thank me later. I was aware I had the freedom to share this correction because I know Steve wants to be God's man more than he wants to be coddled.

Helping each other grow in Christ can mean sharing times of correction as well as times in God's Word. Both are precious moments as deeper unity with Christ draws us more closely into each other than we ever hoped to be.

Each day Steve and I have together as husband and wife is a gift from God that we want to cherish and make the most of. Regardless of how many years or decades God gives us, sadly enough, we know our marriage will come to a close. At the end of our time together my sincere goal is to be able to look at my beloved and say, "I have never had a dearer friend than you. I hope you have felt as loved as you actually are."

A Final Thought

When Steve and I returned from a long trip to South Korea where we were doing some marriage enrichment meetings for couples in the military, I brought home some kind of "bug" that I thought was going to take me out. In my delirium I didn't realize how loud, deep, and life-threatening my coughing sounded to Steve. His fear that I was dying so worried him that he did what any good husband would do…he wrote a song for me. (You thought I was going to say that he brought me a cup of cool water and a cold cloth for my fevered brow, I bet. But, no, he's a songwriter and that's what songwriters do when they are deeply moved.) As unusual as his brand of care was, when he came and sat down on the side of my bed of affliction and announced he'd put his feelings to music, I whispered, "Please sing."

I have to say that the words and the melody soothed my heart like I imagine the songs and sounds David sang and played on his harp did as he ministered to the ailing King Saul. The music was healing to me. More than that, the words washed over me like a tender brush of my loving husband's hand through my hair.

I want to close this book with Steve's song. While it was written about us, we long for these words to apply to your relationship with your spouse. When all is said and done and the span of your marriage is over, we hope what we've offered in these pages inspired you so you too can adopt these lyrics as your own. May God help you love and like each other as you grow closer every day.

Farewell, My Lover

Farewell, my lover
My dearest friend
This walk with you down here—
How sweet it's been

Someday I'll come to where you're going
But until then
I'll miss you, my lover,
My dearest friend

These years with you,
Like hours they have passed
And every mile
Better than the last
Now comes your going;
Much too fast
And I must face my greatest task…to say

Farewell, my lover,
My dearest friend
This walk with you down here—
How sweet it's been

Someday I'll come to where you're going
But until then
I'll miss you, my lover,
My dearest friend [3]

Enhance Your Marriage Questions

Chapter 1: A Decision to Make

1. How much time do you spend with your spouse? What are the biggest hurdles to spending more time together? What areas could you adjust to gain more time with each other?

2. "Anything nice has its price." Discuss some of the costs inherent in gaining more time with your family. Which of these are you willing to pay? Which are too steep?

3. Is Proverbs 31 a blessing or a burden to you as a wife, mother, and woman? Why?

4. Which do you struggle with most as a couple: junk activities, junk expenditures, or too many worthy activities? Discuss a plan that would decrease some of these so you'll have more quality time together.

Chapter 2: Feels like Love

1. We cherish the memories of our most romantic moments, but sometimes it's fun to remember those romantic times that didn't go quite as planned. Share a couple of yours.

2. What were the expectations you had for marriage before you were married? Which have been met? Which are unfulfilled?

3. Gaining a servant's heart includes developing a servant's ear and eye. Think about the times you watch and listen to your spouse. From what you see and hear, what is one thing you think she or he needs more from you?

4. Open communication and sharing continue to be the first steps in reigniting romance. Tell your spouse one thing from your week that he or she may not know.

Chapter 3: Working Together

1. Think about your parents and their interactions. Discuss how much of your expectations for spousal roles comes from what seems "natural" to you. How does this differ from your spouse? How can you resolve any differing expectations?

2. While compromising can sound wonderful, too often it means that neither person is entirely happy with the outcome. What do you think true compromise entails?

3. Mutual edification is an extremely important part of a relationship. Share a time when your spouse modeled Jesus' example through a selfless action.

4. It's important to evaluate how your household runs. Are you both using your gifts effectively in completing the day-to-day tasks? Is there any need to redistribute the workload to better serve each other?

Chapter 4: Excess Baggage

1. At the heart of overcoming wounds is forgiveness. One of the easiest ways to understand true forgiveness is to know how it feels to be forgiven. Share a time when someone forgave you. Now share a time when forgiveness was promised to you but not felt by you. What distinguishes the two events? How can you truly forgive someone?

2. Talk about the letter mentioned in this chapter that touched you the most.

3. Think over your life up to your marriage. Consider the wounds and pain you carry with you from those years. Does your spouse know all or most of them? Why or why not? Contemplate what it would be like to bear each other's burdens with God's help. How can you do this even more? Is this a step you're able and willing to take?

4. This chapter mentions one of the Bible's great promises: freedom in Christ. Have you experienced this freedom? Why do you think it's one of the most amazing gifts God offers?

Chapter 5: Different, Not Difficult

1. Name something you do that you know irritates your spouse. What keeps you from changing this behavior?

2. Sometimes it is the things that first attracted you to your spouse that become sources of irritation later on. Why do you think that is? Can you turn them back into positives?

3. One of the most sensitive of topics is talking about the things that irritate you about your partner. Often simply bringing up the discussion can launch a major argument. How can you guard your conversation and language so you can talk through these important concerns more effectively?

4. How do you decide when to accept a behavior and when to approach your spouse in the hope that he or she will be willing to change?

Chapter 6: God, Marriage, and Money

1. Why do you think money problems are the number one cause of divorce in America?

2. How do you decide what is a "want" and what is a "need" for your household? Do you think your list of needs is the same as your spouse's? If not, what makes them different?

3. One problem in many households is that finances are primarily handled by one partner. Do you both understand your current financial status and goals? Would workshops, seminars, or finance workbooks assist you as a couple?

4. An important lesson to learn is that spending money isn't always the answer for generating romance. Creativity plays an important part. What is one thing you can do for under $10 that will bring a little romance back into your marriage? How can God help you adjust your financial expectations to fit your current lifestyle?

Chapter 7: Staying in Like

1. Best friend. Counselor. Lover. Caretaker. There are a lot of roles we can fulfill for each other, but it becomes dangerous when your spouse fills too many of these. Discuss with each other which roles you want your spouse to fill and which ones can be filled by others in a healthy, marriage-sustaining manner.

2. Time apart is as important for couples as time together. What are some activities and hobbies you think your spouse would find energizing or refreshing to do without you? Can you offer him or her the opportunity to pursue at least one of these this week?

3. Maintaining your self-confidence and self-respect are important components of being a strong partner. What is one new task or undertaking you're interested in pursuing that will enrich your life? When can you schedule it in?

4. Have you set any goals together as a couple? If not, start small. Make a goal you can complete within this week or this month. Continue to set goals together that are designed to draw you closer together and closer to God.

Chapter 8: Protected Love

1. What is your definition of "intimacy"? How does this differ from your spouse's? Do your two definitions fit together or are there conflicts that cause rifts in your communication?

2. Discuss the list about how to safeguard your marriage. Will it work for you? Why or why not? Will you

implement all or part of it? Are there other guidelines you'd like to add?

3. What is the most romantic thing you can think of for your spouse to do for you that doesn't involve sex? Share your ideas, and then discuss whether you can accommodate them and whether you'll give them a try.

4. Second honeymoons are a great idea, but they require planning. What can you do to find time to be together—just you and your mate—this weekend? What can you do during that time that you both would enjoy?

Chapter 9: Customized Love

1. What is the best present your spouse has ever given you? Why did it mean so much?

2. What is one nonsexual way you can say "I love you" to your spouse through actions rather than words or gifts? (Why not keep this to yourself for now and surprise your mate by doing it later this week?)

3. Find a song that reminds you of your spouse and play it for him or her. Explain the connection and how it makes you feel.

4. Being original and personalizing your love takes time, thought, and effort. How much time do you usually devote to thinking about your spouse's needs and desires? Discuss ways to carve out more time to devote to those thoughts so you can avoid falling into ruts for expressing your love.

Chapter 10: The Ships Are Burning...

1. What do you think the most common cause or excuse for "falling out of love" is?

2. A marriage in trouble usually doesn't happen overnight. Often years of small problems build up until their weight topples what was once strong. Even if you feel your marriage is strong, thinking about prevention is a good thing. How can you protect your marriage? If you're down the conflict road a ways, how can you forgive and overcome the frustrations that have built up? Now is the time to take the first step.

3. Sometimes the examples of others can be lights for us. Think of friends and family in marriages you respect. What aspects of their marriages do you most admire? How can you incorporate those to strengthen your marriage?

4. Take a moment right now to pray as a couple over your marriage. If you're not already doing so, make a plan to pray together daily.

Chapter 11: Growing Together

1. What routine do you have for devotions? How do you include your spouse in what you're learning?

2. Why is modeling your faith so important to your family? How can you make faith more dynamic in your family?

3. Have you ever admonished your spouse? How difficult was it? Would you do it differently next time?

4. How can you encourage your spouse's spiritual growth and personal fulfillment? How will this strengthen your marriage?

Notes

Chapter 1: A Decision to Make

1. Steve Chapman, "You Have My Word," © 2010 Steve Chapman, Little Dog Little Boy Music/BMI. Used by permission. All rights reserved.

2. Steve Chapman, "That Way Again," © 2005 Steve Chapman, Times and Seasons/ BMI. Used by permission. All rights reserved.

Chapter 2: Feels like Love

1. Steve Chapman, "We Get in Trouble (When We Kiss)," © 2004 Steve Chapman, Little Dog Little Boy Music/BMI. Used by permission. All rights reserved.

2. Steve and Annie Chapman, "Incompatibility," © 1996 Steve and Annie Chapman, Times and Seasons Music, BMI, on the *Love Was Spoken* CD, S&A Family, Pleasant View, TN. Used by permission. All rights reserved.

3. Steve Chapman, "Feels like Love," © 2003 Steve Chapman, Times and Seasons Music/BMI, on *The Miles* CD, S&A Family, Pleasant View, TN.

Chapter 3: Working Together

1. Steve Chapman, "The Stable," © 1993 Steve Chapman, Times and Seasons Music/ BMI, *Coming Home for Christmas*, CD, S&A Family, Pleasant View, TN. Used by permission. All rights reserved.

Chapter 4: Excess Baggage

1. Sharron Kay King, Steve Chapman, Annie Chapman, "Innocence Lost," © 2012 by Sharron Kay King, Steve Chapman, and Annie Chapman. Published by Songs of

Sharron Music/Little Dog Little Boy Music/BMI. Used by permission. Recorded on Sharron Kay King's CD *The Story of My Life*.

Chapter 6: God, Marriage, and Money

1. From Dave Ramsey's Financial Peace University online resource center, "What Does the Bible Say About Money," https://crc.daveramsey.com/index.cfm?event=dspPast orExt&intContentID=10320, accessed 5/29/13.

2. Ibid.

3. Ibid.

4. Ibid.

5. Dave Ramsey, *The Total Money Makeover* (Nashville: Thomas Nelson, 2009), xxii.

6. Steve Chapman, "My Daddy Needs a Job," © 2010 Steve Chapman, Times and Seasons Music/BMI. Used by permission. All rights reserved.

Chapter 7: Staying in Like

1. Steve and Annie Chapman, "I'm Not Your Mother," © 2009 by Steve and Annie Chapman, Little Dog Little Boy Music/BMI. Used by permission. All rights reserved.

2. Steve Chapman, "Let Me Take Her Home," © 1997 by Steve Chapman, Times and Seasons Music/BMI. Used by permission. All rights reserved.

Chapter 8: Protected Love

1. Tim Alan Gardner, *Sacred Sex* (Colorado Springs: WaterBrook Press, 2002), 48-49.

2. P. Roger Hillerstrom, "The Eroding Effects of Premarital Sex," *The Standard*, December 1984, 13-16. Although this article was written a long time ago, the truths and wisdom are just as pertinent for today's couples.

3. Richard D. Dobbins, PhD, "Helping Teens Wait Until Marriage," *Ministries Today*, March/April 1987, 37-42.

4. Steve Chapman, "Easy to Steal," © 2012 Steve Chapman, Times and Seasons Music/BMI. Used by permission. All rights reserved.

5. Steve Chapman, "Has Been," © 2012 Steve Chapman, Times and Seasons Music/BMI, from the *Finish Well* CD.

Chapter 9: Customized Love

1. Steve Chapman, "When Memories Turn to Gold," © 1991, Steve Chapman, Times and Seasons Music/BMI.

2. Cited in Les and Leslie Parrott, *The One Year Love Talk Devotional for Couples* (Carol Stream, IL: Tyndale Publishers, 2011), January 8.

3. Steve and Annie Chapman, "Come and Walk with Me," © 2012 Steve and Annie Chapman, Little Dog Little Boy Music/BMI. Used by permission. All rights reserved.

Chapter 10: The Ships Are Burning...

1. Steve Chapman, "The Ships Are Burning," © 1991 Steve Chapman, Times and Seasons Music/BMI. Used by permission. All rights reserved.

2. Gary Smalley and John Trent, *The Language of Love* (Pomona, CA: Focus on the Family Publishing, 1988), 87-89.

Chapter 11: Growing Together

1. Charlie and Martha Shedd as quoted in Philip Yancey, *After the Wedding* (Waco, TX: Word Books, 1976), 147-48.

2. *Happiness Is Growing a Marriage,* ed. Gene Van Note (Kansas City, MO: Beacon Hill Press, 1975), 107-08.

3. Steve Chapman, "Farewell, My Lover," © 2008 Steve Chapman, Times and Seasons Music/BMI. Used by permission. All rights reserved.

More Great Books by
Steve Chapman

10 Ways to Prepare Your Son for Life
365 Things Every Hunter Should Know
Another Look at Life from a Deer Stand
The Good Husband's Guide to Balancing Hobbies and Marriage
Great Hunting Stories
Hot Topics for Couples
(with Annie Chapman)
A Hunter Sets His Sights
A Hunter's Cookbook
(with Annie Chapman)
A Look at Life from a Deer Stand
A Look at Life from a Deer Stand Devotional
A Look at Life from a Deer Stand Gift Edition
A Look at Life from a Deer Stand Study Guide
Wasn't It Smart of God To…
With Dad on a Deer Stand
With God on a Deer Hunt

Great Books by Annie Chapman

10 Ways to Prepare Your Daughter for Life
Letting Go of Anger
The Mother-in-Law Dance
Overcoming Negative Emotions
What Every Wife Wants Her Husband to Know

To read sample chapters, go to
www.HarvestHousePublishers.com

More Exciting Harvest House Books by Steve and Annie Chapman

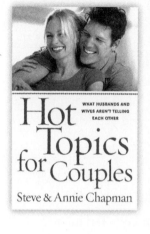

Hot Topics for Couples
Steve and Annie Chapman

What is the greatest challenge of your marriage? What do you and your mate do for fun? Exploring these questions and more, Steve and Annie draw on their 30 years of marriage, God's Word, and a survey of more than 450 couples to explore the truths successful marriages are built on. Through real-life situations, you'll discover important keys to making your marriage stronger, including:

- finding spiritual wholeness
- creating a partnership in love, cooperation, and mutual submission
- recapturing the laughter lost in daily living

As you explore vital topics seldom discussed, your marriage will become deeper and more fulfilling.

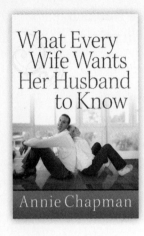

What Every Wife Wants Her Husband to Know
Annie Chapman

With candor and straight talk, Annie explores biblical couples, including Ruth and Boaz and Adam and Eve, and her own marriage to look at vital things you'd like your husband to know but have been reluctant (or too busy) to bring up. She offers innovative and gentle ways to tell your husband:

- I want you to lead me spiritually
- When you help me around the house, I feel loved
- It is important you understand my need to feel financially secure

With godly advice and insights into the covenant of marriage, Annie encourages you to talk with your husband in a way that will improve, heal, or even save your marriage.

Great Hunting Tales and Insights
by Steve Chapman!

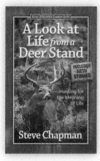

A Look at Life from a Deer Stand

From the incredible rush of bagging "the big one" to standing in awe of God's magnificent creation, Steve Chapman captures the spirit of the hunt. In short chapters filled with excitement and humor, he takes you on his successful and not-so-successful forays into the heart of deer country. As you experience the joy of scouting a trophy buck, you'll discover how the skills necessary for great hunting can help you draw closer to the Lord.

A Look at Life from a Deer Stand Devotional

Just you, God, and a whitetail. Perfect. From the moment he hits the woods to the minute he heads home, avid hunter Steve Chapman revels in the pursuit of whitetails. A vivid storyteller, he invites you to join him in the thickets, meadows, and woods to experience God's magnificent creation and discover powerful truths that reveal the awesome ways He guides you. From the pulse-racing sight of a trophy buck to insights gleaned from a wily doe, these enthusiastic devotions will add to your hunting knowledge as you celebrate God's presence and provision.

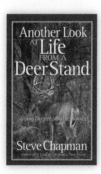

Another Look at Life from a Deer Stand

Drawing on his many years of hunting, avid sportsman Steve takes you to the forests and fields to experience the excitement of sighting whitetails and wily turkeys. From the joys of being the woods to the thrill of handling well-made equipment, you'll relate to the adventure of going after wild game. Along the way you'll also garner some intriguing life truths that will impact your everyday life...spiritual truths that reflect the bounty and grace of the Creator.

Chapman Family Discography

At the Potter's House

An Evening Together

Every Moment

Family Favorites

Finish Well

For Times Like These

Gotta Get There

Hymns from God's Great Cathedral

Kiss of Hearts

Long Enough to Know

Love Was Spoken

The Miles

A Mother's Touch

Nathan Paul

Never Turn Back

The Silver Bridge

That Way Again

This House Still Stands

Tools for the Trade

To find out more about the Chapmans—
their ministry, their music, their recordings—go to
www.SteveandAnnieChapman.com